KETO DIET COOKBOOK
FOR BEGINNERS

1200 Days of Easy-To-Make & Tasty Healthy Recipes with a 30 Days Special Keto Diet Plan to Boost the Immune System and Balance Hormones

Poula Ray

D1637065

Table of Contents

© **Copyright 2022 by Poula Ray - All rights reserved.**

This document is geared towards providing exact and reliable information in regards to the topic and issue covered. The publication is sold with the idea that the publisher is not required to render accounting, officially permitted, or otherwise, qualified services. If advice is necessary, legal or professional, a practiced individual in the profession should be ordered.

- From a Declaration of Principles which was accepted and approved equally by a Committee of the American Bar Association and a Committee of Publishers and Associations.

In no way is it legal to reproduce, duplicate, or transmit any part of this document in either electronic means or in printed format. Recording of this publication is strictly prohibited and any storage of this document is not allowed unless with written permission from the publisher. All rights reserved.

The information provided herein is stated to be truthful and consistent, in that any liability, in terms of inattention or otherwise, by any usage or abuse of any policies, processes, or Instructions: contained within is the solitary and utter responsibility of the recipient reader. Under no circumstances will any legal responsibility or blame be held against the publisher for any reparation, damages, or monetary loss due to the information herein, either directly or indirectly.

Respective authors own all copyrights not held by the publisher.

The information herein is offered for informational purposes solely, and is universal as so. The presentation of the information is without contract or any type of guarantee assurance.

The trademarks that are used are without any consent, and the publication of the trademark is without permission or backing by the trademark owner. All trademarks and brands within this book are for clarifying purposes only and are the owned by the owners themselves, not affiliated with this document.

1. Introduction

The ketogenic diet is trendy, and for an excellent reason. It truly teaches healthy eating without forcing anyone into at risk. A healthy weight allows your body to move freely and your entire internal system to work at its optimal levels.

Cognitive Focus

In order for your brain to work at its best, it needs to have balanced levels of all nutrients and molecules, because a balance allows it to focus on other things, such as working, studying, or creativity. If you eat carbs, the sudden insulin spike that comes with them will force your brain to stop whatever it was doing and to turn its focus on the correct breakdown of glucose molecules. This is why people often feel sleepy and with a foggy mind after high-carb meals. The keto diet keeps the balance strong, so that your brain does not have to deal with any sudden surprises.

Blood Sugar Control

If you already have diabetes, or are prone to it, then controlling your blood sugar is obviously of the utmost importance. However, even if you are not battling a type of diabetes at the moment, that doesn't mean that you are not in danger of developing it in the future. Most people forget that insulin is a finite resource in your body. You are given a certain amount of it, and it is gradually used up throughout your life. The more often you actually eat carbs, the more often your body needs to use insulin to break down the glucose; and when it reaches critically low levels of this finite resource, diabetes is formed.

Lower Cholesterol and Blood Pressure

Cholesterol and triglyceride levels maintain, or ruin, your arterial health. If your arteries are actually clogged up with cholesterol, they cannot efficiently transfer blood through your system, which in some cases even results in heart attacks. The keto diet keeps all of these levels at an optimal level, so that they do not interfere with your body's normal functioning.

Chapter 1:   Breakfast Recipes

Recipe 1:   Almond Pancakes

Serving Size: 2

Cooking Time: 15 minutes

Ingredients:

- ½ cup almond flour
- 1 egg
- 2 ½ tablespoons unsweetened almond milk
- 2 tablespoons coconut oil, divided
- 1 tablespoon erythritol (optional; use if you want sweet taste)
- Pinch salt (if using sweetener)
- ½ teaspoon baking powder
- ½ teaspoon pure vanilla extract (optional)

Directions:

1. In a bowl, put and mix all the ingredients except 1 tablespoon of coconut oil with a whisk until smooth.
2. Place an oiled pan over medium-low heat. Pour heaping tablespoons of batter onto the pan and form pancakes.
3. Cover and fry about 1-2 minutes, then flip pancakes when bubbles start to form and cook another 1-2 minutes.
4. Transfer pancakes to the plate and repeat the cooking process until the batter is used up.
5. Serve whipped cream or sour cream and berries (do not forget about carbs in berries and cream).

Nutritional Value: Calories 325; Fat 30g; Carbohydrates 7g; Protein 9g

Recipe 2: Avocado Boats with Tuna Mayo

Serving Size: 4

Cooking Time: 10 minutes

Ingredients:

- 2 large avocados
- ½ teaspoon salt
- ½ teaspoon pepper
- 10 tablespoons mayonnaise
- 1 cup of canned tuna
- 1 fresh onion, thinly chopped

Directions:

1. In a large-sized bowl mix the mayonnaise and tuna. Season with salt and pepper.
2. Cut the prepared avocado into halves and remove the pit. Then fill the center with the mayo mixture.
3. Sprinkle immediately with the fresh onion and serve.

Nutritional Value: Calories 346; Fat 27g; Carbohydrates 8g; Protein 14g

Recipe 3:   Bacon and Lemon Breakfast Muffins

Serving Size: 12

Cooking Time: 20 minutes

Ingredients:

- 1 cup bacon, finely chopped
- Salt and black pepper to the taste
- ½ cup ghee, melted
- 3 cups almond flour
- 1 teaspoon baking soda
- 4 eggs
- 2 teaspoons lemon thyme

Directions:

1. In a bowl, mix flour with baking soda and eggs and stir well.
2. Add ghee, lemon thyme, bacon, salt and pepper and whisk well.
3. Divide this into a lined muffin pan, introduce in the oven at 350 degrees F and bake for 20 minutes.
4. Leave muffins to cool down a bit, divide on plates and serve them.
5. Enjoy!

Nutritional Value: Calories 213; Fat 7g; Carbohydrates 9g; Protein 8g

Recipe 4: Baked Granola

Serving Size: 4

Cooking Time: 55 minutes

Ingredients:

- ½ cup almonds, chopped
- 1 cup pecans, chopped
- ½ cup walnuts, chopped
- ½ cup coconut, flaked
- ¼ cup flax meal
- ½ cup almond milk
- ¼ cup sunflower seeds
- ¼ cup pepitas
- ½ cup stevia
- ¼ cup ghee, melted
- 1 teaspoon honey
- 1 teaspoon vanilla
- 1 teaspoon cinnamon, ground
- A pinch of salt
- ½ teaspoon nutmeg
- ¼ cup water

Directions:

1. In a bowl, mix almonds with pecans, walnuts, coconut, flax meal, milk, sunflower seeds, pepitas, stevia, ghee, honey, vanilla, cinnamon, salt, nutmeg and water and whisk very well.
2. Grease a baking sheet with parchment paper, spread granola mix and press well.
3. Cover with another piece of parchment paper, introduce in the oven at 250 degrees F and bake for 1 hour.
4. Take granola out of the oven, leave aside to cool down, break into pieces and serve.
5. Enjoy!

Nutritional Value: Calories 340; Fat 32g; Carbohydrates 8g; Protein 20g

Recipe 5: Basil Mozzarella Eggs

Serving Size: 4

Cooking Time: 20 minutes

Ingredients:

- 2 tablespoons butter, melted
- 6 teaspoons basil pesto
- 1 cup mozzarella cheese, grated
- 6 eggs, whisked
- 2 tablespoons basil, chopped
- A pinch of salt and black pepper

Directions:

1. In a bowl, put and combine all the ingredients except the butter and whisk them well.
2. Preheat your Air Fryer at 360 degrees F, drizzle the butter on the bottom, spread the eggs mix, cook for 20 minutes, and serve for breakfast.

Nutritional Value: Calories 207; Fat 14g; Carbohydrates 4g; Protein 8g

Recipe 6: Bell Peppers and Avocado Bowls

Serving Size: 4

Cooking Time: 15 minutes

Ingredients:

- 2 tablespoons olive oil
- 2 shallots, chopped1 red bell pepper, cut into strips
- 1 yellow bell pepper, cut into strips
- 1 green bell pepper, cut into strips
- 1 big avocado, peeled, pitted and cut into wedges
- 1 teaspoon sweet paprika
- ½ cup vegetable stock
- Salt and black pepper to the taste
- 1 tablespoon chives, chopped

Directions:

1. Heat up a pan with the oil medium heat, add the shallots and sauté them for 2 minutes.
2. Add the bell peppers, avocado and the other ingredients except the chives, toss, bring to a simmer and cook over medium heat for 13 minutes more.
3. Add the chives, toss, divide into bowls and serve for breakfast.

Nutritional Value: Calories 194; Fat 17.1g; Carbohydrates 6.6g; Protein 2g

Recipe 7: Breakfast Buttered Eggs

Serving Size: 2

Cooking Time: 15 minutes

Ingredients:

- 1 tablespoon coconut oil
- 2 tablespoon butter
- 1 teaspoon fresh thyme
- 4 eggs
- 2 garlic cloves, minced
- ½ cup chopped parsley
- ½ cup chopped cilantro
- ¼ teaspoon cumin
- ¼ teaspoon cayenne pepper
- Salt and black pepper, to taste

Directions:

1. Drizzle the coconut oil into a non-stick skillet over a heat of medium heat. Once the prepared oil is warm, add the butter, and melt. Add garlic and thyme and cook for 30 seconds. Sprinkle with parsley and cilantro; and cook for another 2 minutes, until crisp.
2. Carefully crack the eggs into the skillet. Lower the heat and cook for 4-6 minutes. Season with salt, black pepper, cumin, and cayenne pepper. When the eggs are just set, turn the heat off and transfer to a serving plate.

Nutritional Value: Calories 321; Fat 21.5g; Carbohydrates 2.5g; Protein 12.8g

Recipe 8: Breakfast Meatloaf

Serving Size: 4

Cooking Time: 35 minutes

Ingredients:

- 1 teaspoon ghee
- 1 small yellow onion, chopped
- 1 pound sweet sausage, chopped
- 6 eggs
- 1 cup cheddar cheese, shredded
- 4 ounces cream cheese, soft
- Salt and black pepper to the taste
- 2 tablespoons scallions, chopped

Directions:

1. In a large-sized bowl, mix eggs with salt, pepper, onion, sausage and half of the cream and whisk well.
2. Grease a meatloaf with the ghee, pour sausage and eggs mix, introduce in the oven at 350 degrees F and bake for 30 minutes.
3. Take meatloaf out of the oven, leave aside for a couple of minutes, spread the rest of the cream cheese on top and sprinkle scallions and cheddar cheese all over.
4. Introduce meatloaf in the oven again and bake for 5 minutes more.
5. After the time has passed, broil meatloaf for 3 minutes, leave it aside to cool down a bit, slice and serve it.
6. Enjoy!

Nutritional Value: Calories 560; Fat 32g; Carbohydrates 6g; Protein 45g

Recipe 9: Brussels Sprouts Delight

Serving Size: 3

Cooking Time: 12 minutes

Ingredients:

- 3 eggs
- Salt and black pepper to the taste
- 1 tablespoon ghee, melted
- 2 shallots, minced
- 2 garlic cloves, minced
- 12 ounces Brussels sprouts, thinly sliced
- 2 ounces bacon, chopped
- 1 and ½ tablespoons apple cider vinegar

Directions:

1. Heat up a large-sized pan over medium heat, add bacon, stir, cook until it's crispy, transfer to a plate and leave aside for now.
2. Heat up the large-sized pan again over medium heat, add shallots and garlic, stir and cook for 30 seconds.
3. Add Brussels sprouts, salt, pepper and apple cider vinegar, stir and cook for 5 minutes.
4. Return bacon to pan, stir and cook for 5 minutes more.
5. Add ghee, stir and make a hole in the center.
6. Crack eggs into the pan, cook until they are done and serve right away.
7. Enjoy!

Nutritional Value: Calories 240; Fat 7g; Carbohydrates 7g; Protein 12g

Recipe 10: Cauliflower Omelet

Serving Size: 4

Cooking Time: 15 minutes

Ingredients:

- 4 eggs, whisked
- 1 cup cauliflower florets, chopped
- 2 spring onions, chopped
- 1 tablespoon olive oil
- ½ cup heavy cream
- ½ teaspoon sweet paprikaSalt and black pepper to the taste
- 1 tablespoon chives, chopped

Directions:

1. Heat up a large-sized pan with the oil over medium heat, add the onion and the cauliflower, stir and sauté for 5 minutes.
2. Add the eggs mixed with the cream, paprika, salt and pepper, toss, spread into the pan, cook over medium heat for 10 minutes, divide between plates, sprinkle the chives on top and serve.

Nutritional Value: Calories 200; Fat 4g; Carbohydrates 5g; Protein 10g

Recipe 11: Cauliflower Patties

Serving Size: 2

Cooking Time: 15 minutes

Ingredients:

- 10 oz. cauliflower
- 1 tablespoon yeast
- 2/3 cup almond flour
- ½ teaspoon cumin powder
- ½ teaspoon paprika
- 2 eggs
- 2 tablespoon ghee butter
- Salt and pepper to taste

Directions:

1. Divide the cauliflower into florets, put them in a pot and boil for 8-10 min.
2. Remove to a plate and let it rest for 3-4 min.
3. Meanwhile, in a bowl combine the eggs, paprika, cumin, yeast, pepper, salt.
4. Put the cauliflower in a blender and pulse till even.
5. Add the cauliflower to the bowl with other mixed ingredients, mix well and form the patties.
6. Heat the ghee butter in a skillet over medium heat, cook the patties for 3-5 min per side.

Nutritional Value: Calories 235; Fat 23g; Carbohydrates 5g; Protein 6g

Recipe 12: Cheese and Aioli Eggs

Serving Size: 8

Cooking Time: 20 minutes

Ingredients:

- 8 eggs, hard-boiled, chopped
- 28 ozs. tuna in brine, drained
- ½ cup lettuces, torn into pieces
- ½ cup green onions, finely chopped
- ½ cup feta cheese, crumbled
- ⅓ cup sour cream
- ½ tablespoon mustard

For Aioli:
- 1 cup mayonnaise
- 2 cloves garlic, minced
- 1 tablespoon lemon juice
- Salt and black pepper, to taste

Directions:

1. Set the eggs in a serving bowl. Place in tuna, onion, mustard, cheese, lettuce, and sour cream.
2. To prepare aioli, mix in a bowl mayonnaise, lemon juice, and garlic. Add in black pepper and salt. Stir in the prepared aioli to the bowl to incorporate everything. Serve with pickles.

Nutritional Value: Calories 355; Fat 22.5g; Carbohydrates 1.8g; Protein 29.5g

Recipe 13: Cheese and Oregano Muffins

Serving Size: 6

Cooking Time: 25 minutes

Ingredients:

- 2 tablespoons olive oil
- 1 egg
- 2 tablespoons parmesan cheese
- ½ teaspoon oregano, dried
- 1 cup almond flour
- ¼ teaspoon baking soda
- Salt and black pepper to the taste
- ½ cup coconut milk
- 1 cup cheddar cheese, grated

Directions:

1. In a bowl, mix flour with oregano, salt, pepper, parmesan and baking soda and stir.
2. In another bowl, mix coconut milk with egg and olive oil and stir well.
3. Combine the 2 mixtures and whisk well.
4. Add cheddar cheese, stir, pour this a lined muffin tray, introduce in the oven at 350 degrees F for 25 minutes.
5. Leave your muffins to cool down for a few minutes, divide them on plates and serve.
6. Enjoy!

Nutritional Value: Calories 160; Fat 3g; Carbohydrates 6g; Protein 10g

Recipe 14: Cheesy Ham and Chive Roll-Ups

Serving Size: 2

Cooking Time: 10 minutes

Ingredients:

- 3 oz. cream cheese; at room temperature.
- 6 slices Black Forest ham {about 5 oz. total}
- ¼ cup shredded Monterey Jack cheese.
- 1 tablespoon chopped fresh chives
- ½ teaspoon onion powder.
- ½ teaspoon garlic powder
- ⅛ teaspoon freshly ground black pepper.
- ⅛ teaspoon salt

Directions:

1. On a cutting board, lay out the six ham slices. Spread ½ oz. of cream cheese on each ham slice, covering evenly
2. Distribute the chives evenly over each piece of ham. Top evenly with the Monterey Jack cheese.
3. Sprinkle each piece with the garlic powder, onion powder, pepper and salt
4. Roll up each slice and enjoy. If desired, slice each roll crosswise into 1-inch pieces and serve.

Nutritional Value: Calories 345; Fat 26.5g; Carbohydrates 5.7g; Protein 21.1g

Recipe 15: Chili Bacon and Eggs

Serving Size: 4

Cooking Time: 10 minutes

Ingredients:

- 1 Jalapenos, sliced. with seeds removed
- 12 slices back bacon.
- 3-oz. chopped onion
- 5-oz. red bell pepper, chopped.
- 8 large eggs
- Oil for frying

Directions:

1. Fry the onion, pepper and chili in a skillet until tender but not brown. Chop the bacon finely in a processor or by hand.
2. Add to the vegetable mixture and fry until the bacon is crisp. Fry the eggs.
3. Divide the bacon mixture among 4 plates and top each portion with 2 fried eggs.

Nutritional Value: Calories 310; Fat 17.5g; Carbohydrates 6.3g; Protein 30.8g

Recipe 16: Coleslaw with Eggs

Serving Size: 4

Cooking Time: 15 minutes

Ingredients:

- 3 cups cabbage, shredded
- 2 large eggs, boiled
- 1 ½ tablespoon Dijon Mustard
- ½ cup mayonnaise
- ½ teaspoon salt
- ½ teaspoon pepper
- 2 tablespoons fresh parsley, chopped
- 1 teaspoon poppy seeds
- 1 tablespoon white vinegar

Directions:

1. In a small bowl prepare dressing by mixing the Dijon mustard, mayonnaise and white vinegar. Set aside.
2. Peel the eggs and chop them. Then in a large bowl mix the shredded cabbage, chopped parsley and chopped eggs.
3. Stir in the prepared dressing and combine well. Season with salt, pepper and poppy seeds.
4. Put in the refrigerator for 1 hour before serving. Serve cold and enjoy!

Nutritional Value: Calories 167; Fat 13g; Carbohydrates 4.3g; Protein 6.8g

Recipe 17: Creamy Eggs

Serving Size: 4

Cooking Time: 15 minutes

Ingredients:

- 8 eggs, whisked
- 2 spring onions, chopped
- 1 tablespoon olive oil
- ½ cup heavy cream
- Salt and black pepper to the taste
- ½ cup mozzarella, shredded
- 1 tablespoon chives, chopped

Directions:

1. Heat up a large-sized pan with the oil over medium heat, add the spring onions, toss and sauté them for 3 minutes.
2. Add the eggs mixed with the cream, salt and pepper and stir into the pan.
3. Sprinkle the mozzarella, on top, cook the mix for 12 minutes, divide it between plates, sprinkle the chives on top and serve.

Nutritional Value: Calories 220; Fat 18.5g; Carbohydrates 1.8g; Protein 12.5g

Recipe 18: Egg and Bacon Stuffed Avocados

Serving Size: 2

Cooking Time: 15 minutes

Ingredients:

- 2 large avocados.
- 4 large eggs
- 4 strips cooked sugar-free bacon, crumbled.
- ¼-teaspoon sea salt
- ¼-teaspoon black pepper

Directions:

1. Preheat oven to 400 degrees F. Cut avocados in half lengthwise and remove the pit. Scoop some avocado out of each half to create a well.
2. Sprinkle 1 strip crumbled bacon into each avocado well. Crack 1 egg directly into each avocado half. Season with black pepper and salt
3. Place avocados on a baking sheet. Bake for approximately about 15 minutes or until egg is cooked to desired doneness.

Nutritional Value: Calories 478; Fat 35.1g; Carbohydrates 13.1g; Protein 23.1g

Recipe 19: Feta Omelet

Serving Size: 1

Cooking Time: 10 minutes

Ingredients:

- 3 eggs
- 1 tablespoon ghee
- 1 ounce feta cheese, crumbled
- 1 tablespoon heavy cream
- 1 tablespoon jarred pesto
- Salt and black pepper to the taste

Directions:

1. In a bowl, mix eggs with heavy cream, salt and pepper and whisk well.
2. Heat up a large-sized pan with the ghee over medium high heat, add whisked eggs, spread into the pan and cook your omelet until it's fluffy.
3. Sprinkle cheese and spread pesto on your omelet, fold in half, cover pan and cook for 5 minutes more.
4. Transfer omelet to a plate and serve.
5. Enjoy!

Nutritional Value: Calories 500; Fat 43g; Carbohydrates 3g; Protein 30g

Recipe 20: Hot Dog Rolls

Serving Size: 4

Cooking Time: 20 minutes

Ingredients:

- 4 hot dogs
- ¾ cup almond flour.
- 1 egg
- 1 ½ cups shredded mozzarella cheese.
- 2 tablespoon cream cheese; at room temperature
- 1 teaspoon Italian seasoning.
- 1 teaspoon minced garlic

Directions:

1. Preheat your oven to 425-Degrees F. In a large microwaveable bowl, combine the mozzarella cheese and cream cheese. Microwave on high for 1 minute. Remove, stir and microwave again for 30 seconds more. The mixture will be very hot.
2. Now, add the almond flour, egg, garlic and Italian seasoning to the cheese mixture. Stir to incorporate fully
3. With wet hands, divide the dough into four equal pieces. Shape one piece of dough around each hot dog, encasing the hot dog completely
4. Place the dough-wrapped hot dogs onto a parchment-lined baking sheet. Use a fork to poke holes into each piece of dough so it doesn't bubble up during cooking. Put the prepared baking sheet into the preheated oven. Bake for 7 to 8 minutes.
5. Remove the tray from the oven. Check for bubbles {prick with a fork, if formed}. Turn the dogs over. Return to the oven for another 6 to 7 minutes.
6. Remove the sheet from the oven. Cool the hot dog rolls for 3 to 5 minutes before serving.

Nutritional Value: Calories 435; Fat 34.7g; Carbohydrates 7.6g; Protein 18.6g

Recipe 21: Kale Frittata

Serving Size: 4

Cooking Time: 30 minutes

Ingredients:

- 8 eggs, whisked
- 2 shallots, chopped
- 1 tablespoon avocado oil
- 1 cup kale, torn
- Salt and black pepper to the taste
- ¼ cup mozzarella, shredded
- 2 tablespoons chives, chopped

Directions:

1. Heat up a large-sized pan with the oil over medium heat, add the shallots, stir and cook for 5 minutes.
2. Add the kale, stir and cook for 4 minutes more.
3. Add the eggs mixed with the mozzarella, spread into the pan, sprinkle the chives on top and bake at 390 degrees F for 20 minutes.
4. Divide the frittata between plates and serve.

Nutritional Value: Calories 140; Fat 6.7g; Carbohydrates 4.3g; Protein 10g

Recipe 22: Mushroom and Cheese Lettuce Wraps

Serving Size: 4

Cooking Time: 20 minutes

Ingredients:

For the Wraps:
- 6 eggs
- 2 tablespoon almond milk
- 1 tablespoon olive oil
- Sea salt, to taste

For the Filling:
- 1 teaspoon olive oil
- 1 cup mushrooms, chopped
- Salt and black pepper, to taste
- ½ teaspoon cayenne pepper
- 8 fresh lettuce leaves
- 4 slices gruyere cheese
- 2 tomatoes, sliced

Directions:

1. Mix all the ingredients for the wraps thoroughly.
2. Set a frying pan over medium heat. Add in ¼ of the mixture and cook for 4 minutes on both sides. Do the same thrice and set the wraps aside, they should be kept warm.
3. In a separate pan over medium heat, warm 1 teaspoon of olive oil. Cook the mushrooms for 5 minutes until soft; add cayenne pepper, black pepper, and salt. Set 1-2 lettuce leaves onto every wrap, split the mushrooms among the wraps and top with tomatoes and cheese.

Nutritional Value: Calories 147.2; Fat 44g; Carbohydrates 5.4g; Protein 19.5g

Recipe 23: Ricotta Cloud Pancakes with Whipped Cream

Serving Size: 4

Cooking Time: 10 minutes

Ingredients:

- 1 cup almond flour
- 1 teaspoon baking powder
- 2 ½ tablespoon swerve
- ⅓ teaspoon salt
- 1 ¼ cups ricotta cheese
- ⅓ cup coconut milk
- 2 large eggs
- 1 cup heavy whipping cream

Directions:

1. In a large-sized bowl, whisk the almond flour, baking powder, swerve, and salt. Set aside.
2. Crack the eggs into the blender and process on medium speed for 30 seconds. Add the ricotta cheese, continue processing it, and gradually pour the coconut milk in while you keep on blending. in about 90 seconds, the mixture will be creamy and smooth. Pour it into the dry ingredients and whisk to combine.
3. Set a skillet over medium heat and let it heat for a minute. Then, fetch a soup spoonful of mixture into the skillet and cook it for 1 minute.
4. Flip the pancake and cook further for 1 minute. Remove onto a plate and repeat the cooking process until the batter is exhausted. Serve the pancakes with whipping cream.

Nutritional Value: Calories 407; Fat 30.6g; Carbohydrates 6.6g; Protein 11.5g

Recipe 24: Sausage Egg Cups

Serving Size: 6

Cooking Time: 40 minutes

Ingredients:

- ½-lb. ground pork
- 12 large eggs
- 1 large avocado, peeled and diced.
- ¼-medium yellow onion, chopped.
- ¼-cup zucchini, chopped.
- Coconut oil to grease muffin tin.
- ½-teaspoon dried sage
- ¼-teaspoon red pepper flakes
- ½-teaspoon salt.
- ½-teaspoon black pepper

Directions:

1. Preheat oven to a heat of 350 degrees F. Heat a large skillet over medium heat and add ground pork, sage, salt, black pepper and red pepper flakes. Cook until meat is no longer pink
2. Now, remove pork mixture with a slotted spoon and set aside.
3. Add onion and zucchini to pan and sauté until tender; about 4 minutes. Add cooked onion and zucchini to pork mixture in a medium bowl
4. Add eggs to pork mixture and stir until combined. Oil each well of a 12-cup muffin tin with a small amount of coconut oil and pour mixture evenly into each well.
5. Bake for 30 minutes or until egg is cooked through. Top each egg cup with a few pieces of avocado.

Nutritional Value: Calories 227; Fat 13.1g; Carbohydrates 3.5g; Protein 20.3g

Recipe 25: Sausage Stuffed Bell Peppers

Serving Size: 4

Cooking Time: 5 hours

Ingredients:

- 1 cup breakfast sausage, crumbled
- 4 bell peppers, seedless and cut the top
- ½ cup coconut milk
- 6 eggs
- 1 cup cheddar cheese, shredded

From the cupboard:

- 1 tablespoon extra-virgin olive oil
- ½ teaspoon freshly ground black pepper

Directions:

1. Add the coconut milk, eggs, and black pepper in a medium bowl, whisking until smooth. Set aside.
2. Line your slow cooker insert with aluminum foil. Grease the aluminum foil with 1 tablespoon olive oil.
3. Evenly stuff four bell peppers with the crumbled sausage and spoon the egg mixture into the peppers.
4. Arrange the stuffed peppers in the slow cooker. Sprinkle the cheese on top.
5. Cook covered on LOW for 4 t0 5 hours, or until the peppers are browned and the eggs are completely set.
6. Divide in 4 serving plates and serve warm.

Nutritional Value: Calories 459; Fat 36.3g; Carbohydrates 7.9g; Protein 25.2g

Recipe 26: Shrimp and Olives Pan

Serving Size: 4

Cooking Time: 10 minutes

Ingredients:

- 1 pound shrimp, peeled and deveined
- 1 cup black olives, pitted and halved
- ½ cup kalamata olives, pitted and halved
- 2 spring onions, chopped
- 2 teaspoons sweet paprika
- 1 tablespoon olive oil
- Salt and black pepper to the taste
- ½ cup heavy cream

Directions:

1. Heat up a large-sized pan with the oil over medium heat, add the onions, toss and cook for 2 minutes.
2. Add the shrimp and the other ingredients except the cream, toss and cook for 4 minutes more.
3. Add the cream, toss, cook over medium heat for another 4 minutes, divide everything between plates and serve for breakfast.

Nutritional Value: Calories 263; Fat 14.8g; Carbohydrates 5.5g; Protein 26.7g

Recipe 27: Spiced Eggs

Serving Size: 4

Cooking Time: 20 minutes

Ingredients:

- 1 tablespoon avocado oil
- 2 spring onions, chopped
- 1 tablespoon cilantro, chopped
- 4 eggs, whisked
- 1 teaspoon cumin, ground
- 1 teaspoon allspice, ground
- 1 teaspoon nutmeg, ground
- Salt and black pepper to the taste
- 1 tablespoons parsley, chopped

Directions:

1. Heat up a large-sized pan with the oil over medium heat, add the spring onions, stir and cook for 2 minutes.
2. Add the eggs and the other ingredients, stir, spread into the pan and cook over medium heat for 13 minutes.
3. Divide the eggs between plates and serve for breakfast.

Nutritional Value: Calories 150; Fat 6g; Carbohydrates 10g; Protein 12g

Recipe 28: Spicy Egg Muffins with Bacon and Cheese

Serving Size: 6

Cooking Time: 30 minutes

Ingredients:

- 12 eggs
- ¼ cup coconut milk
- Salt and black pepper to taste
- 1 cup grated cheddar cheese
- 12 slices bacon
- 4 jalapeño peppers, seeded and minced

Directions:

1. Preheat oven to 370°F.
2. Crack the eggs into a large-sized bowl and whisk with coconut milk until combined. Season with salt and pepper, and evenly stir in the cheddar cheese.
3. Line each hole of a muffin tin with a slice of bacon and fill each with the egg mixture two-thirds way up. Top with the jalapeno peppers and bake in the oven for 18 to 20 minutes or until puffed and golden. Remove, allow cooling for a few minutes, and serve with arugula salad.

Nutritional Value: Calories 302; Fat 23.7g; Carbohydrates 3.2g; Protein 20g

Recipe 29: Spicy Scrambled Eggs

Serving Size: 3

Cooking Time: 15 minutes

Ingredients:

- 1 tablespoon olive oil
- 2 scallions, chopped
- 6 eggs
- 1/3 cup full-fat milk
- 1/2 teaspoon chili powder
- salt and pepper, to taste

Directions:

1. Heat the olive oil in a large-sized nonstick skillet over a moderate flame. Then, fry the scallions until just tender and fragrant.
2. In a mixing dish, whisk the eggs with the milk and chili powder. Pour the egg mixture into the skillet and shake the pan to spread the ingredients evenly.
3. Cook the eggs for approximately about 4 to 5 minutes or until set. Season with salt and black pepper; adjust the seasonings and serve warm. Bon appétit!

Nutritional Value: Calories 317; Fat 24.3g; Carbohydrates 3.8g; Protein 19g

Recipe 30: Zucchini and Bacon Hash

Serving Size: 2

Cooking Time: 30 minutes

Ingredients:

- 2 tablespoons butter, divided
- 1 garlic clove, finely chopped
- 2 bacon slices, chopped
- 1 medium zucchini, cut into medium pieces
- 1 tablespoon fresh parsley, chopped
- 1 large organic egg
- Salt, as required

Directions:

1. In a skillet, melt one tablespoon of butter over medium heat and sauté the garlic for about one minute.
2. Add the bacon slices and cook for about 7-8 minutes or until lightly browned, stirring frequently.
3. Add the zucchini and cook for about 10-15 minutes, stirring occasionally.
4. Meanwhile, in a large nonstick frying pan, melt the remaining butter over medium heat.
5. Carefully, crack the egg into frying pan and cook for about 2-2½ minutes, gently tilting the pan occasionally.
6. In the skillet of zucchini, stir in the salt and remove from heat.
7. Transfer the zucchini hash onto a serving plate and top with the egg.
8. Sprinkle the egg with a little salt.
9. Garnish with fresh parsley and serve.

Nutritional Value: Calories 614; Fat 52.5g; Carbohydrates 4.9g; Protein 29.7g

Chapter 2:   Lunch Recipes

Recipe 31: Bacon Wrapped Chicken

Serving Size: 4

Cooking Time: 35 minutes

Ingredients:

- 1 tablespoon chives, chopped
- 8 ounces cream cheese
- 2 pounds chicken breasts, skinless and boneless
- 12 bacon slices
- Salt and black pepper to the taste

Directions:

1. Heat up a large-sized pan over medium heat, add bacon, cook until it's half done, transfer to paper towels and drain grease.
2. In a large-sized bowl, mix cream cheese with salt, pepper and chives and stir.
3. Use a meat tenderizer to flatten chicken breasts well, divide cream cheese mix, roll them up and wrap each in a cooked bacon slice.
4. Arrange wrapped chicken breasts into a baking dish, introduce in the oven at 375 degrees F and bake for 30 minutes.
5. Divide on plates and serve.
6. Enjoy!

Nutritional Value: Calories 700; Fat 45g; Carbohydrates 5g; Protein 45g

Recipe 32: Baked Tofu with Roasted Peppers

Serving Size: 4

Cooking Time: 20 minutes

Ingredients:

- 3 oz dairy-free cream cheese
- ¾ cup vegan mayonnaise
- 2 oz cucumber, diced
- 1 large tomato, chopped
- Salt and black pepper to taste
- 2 teaspoon dried parsley
- 4 orange bell peppers
- 2 ½ cups cubed tofu
- 1 tablespoon melted vegan butter
- 1 teaspoon dried basil

Directions:

1. Preheat a broiler to 450 F and line a baking sheet with parchment paper. in a salad bowl, combine cream cheese, vegan mayonnaise, cucumber, tomato, salt, pepper, and parsley; refrigerate.
2. Arrange bell peppers and tofu on the paper-lined baking sheet, drizzle with melted butter, and season with basil, salt, and pepper. Use hands to rub the ingredients until evenly coated. Bake for 15 minutes until the peppers have charred lightly and the tofu browned.

Nutritional Value: Calories 840; Fat 76g; Carbohydrates 8g; Protein 28g

Recipe 33: Balsamic Steaks

Serving Size: 4

Cooking Time: 15 minutes

Ingredients:

- 1 pound beef steaks, cut into 4 sliced
- 2 tablespoons olive oil
- Salt and black pepper to the taste
- ¼ cup balsamic vinegar
- 2 garlic cloves, minced
- 1 teaspoon red pepper flakes
- 1 teaspoon garlic powder
- 2 shallots, chopped
- 1 tablespoon chives, chopped

Directions:

1. Heat up a pan with the oil over medium heat, add the garlic, shallots, pepper flakes and garlic powder, stir and sauté for 5 minutes.
2. Add the steaks and the other ingredients, cook them for 5 minutes on each side, divide between plates and serve.

Nutritional Value: Calories 435; Fat 23g; Carbohydrates 10g; Protein 35g

Recipe 34: Beef Curry

Serving Size: 4

Cooking Time: 45 minutes

Ingredients:

- 2 tablespoons olive oil
- 1 pound beef stew meat, cubed
- 2 shallots, chopped
- 1 cup beef stock
- 2 cups coconut milk
- 1 tablespoon lime juice
- 3 garlic cloves, minced
- 1 tablespoon cilantro, chopped
- 1 tablespoon ginger, grated
- 2 tablespoons red curry paste
- 1 teaspoon turmeric, ground
- 1 teaspoon cumin, ground

Directions:

1. Heat up a pot with the oil over medium high heat, add the shallots, garlic and the ginger, stir and sauté for 5 minutes.
2. Add the meat and the curry paste, toss and brown for 5 minutes more.
3. Add the stock and the other ingredients, bring to a simmer and cook over medium heat for 35 minutes, stirring often.
4. Divide the curry into bowls and serve for lunch.

Nutritional Value: Calories 430; Fat 22g; Carbohydrates 7g; Protein 23g

Recipe 35: Beef with Kale and Leeks

Serving Size: 4

Cooking Time: 30 minutes

Ingredients:

- 2 tablespoons olive oil
- 1 pound beef stew meat, cubed
- 1 cup kale, torn
- 2 leeks, chopped
- 1 cup tomato passata
- A pinch of salt and black pepper
- 1 tablespoon cilantro, chopped
- 1 teaspoon sweet paprika
- ½ teaspoon rosemary, dried

Directions:

1. Heat up a large-sized pan with the oil over medium heat, add the leeks and the meat and brown for 5 minutes.
2. Add the rest of the prepared ingredients, bring to a simmer and cook over medium heat for 25 minutes more.
3. Divide everything into bowls and serve.

Nutritional Value: Calories 250; Fat 5g; Carbohydrates 3g; Protein 12g

Recipe 36: Chicken and Bacon Pie

Serving Size: 4

Cooking Time: 55 minutes

Ingredients:

- ¾ cup Greek yogurt
- 1 sweet onion, chopped
- 3 oz bacon, chopped
- 3 tablespoon butter
- 1 carrot, chopped
- 3 garlic cloves, minced
- Salt and black pepper, to taste
- ½ cup chicken stock
- ½ lb chicken breasts, cubed
- ¾ cup mozzarella, shredded

For the dough
- ¾ cup almond flour
- 2 tablespoon cottage cheese
- 2 cups mozzarella, shredded
- 1 egg
- 1 teaspoon onion powder
- 1 teaspoon garlic powder

Directions:

1. Preheat oven to 370 F. Sauté onion, garlic, pepper, bacon, salt, and carrot for 5 minutes in warm butter. Add in chicken and cook for 3 minutes. Stir in Greek yogurt and stock and cook for 7 minutes. Add in ¾ cup mozzarella cheese and set aside. Microwave mozzarella and cottage cheeses from the dough Ingredients1 minute.
2. Stir in garlic powder, almond flour, onion powder, and egg. Knead the dough well, split into 4 pieces, and flatten each into a circle. Set the chicken mixture into 4 ramekins, top each with a dough circle, and bake for 25 minutes. Serve.

Nutritional Value: Calories 503; Fat 31g; Carbohydrates 5.6g; Protein 40.9g

Recipe 37: Chicken Calzone

Serving Size: 12

Cooking Time: 1 hour

Ingredients:

- 2 eggs
- 1 keto pizza crust
- ½ cup parmesan, grated
- 1 pound chicken breasts, skinless, boneless and each sliced in halves
- ½ cup keto marinara sauce
- 1 teaspoon Italian seasoning
- 1 teaspoon onion powder
- 1 teaspoon garlic powder
- Salt and black pepper to the taste
- ¼ cup flaxseed, ground
- 8 ounces provolone cheese

Directions:

1. In a bowl, mix Italian seasoning with onion powder, garlic powder, salt, pepper, flaxseed and parmesan and stir well.
2. In another bowl, mix eggs with a pinch of salt and pepper and whisk well.
3. Dip chicken pieces in eggs and then in seasoning mix, place all pieces on a lined baking sheet and bake in the oven at 350 degrees F for 30 minutes.
4. Put pizza crust dough on a lined baking sheet and spread half of the provolone cheese on half
5. Take chicken out of the oven, chop and spread over provolone cheese.
6. Add marinara sauce and then the rest of the cheese.
7. Cover all these with the other half of the dough and shape your calzone.
8. Seal its edges, introduce in the oven at 350 degrees F and bake for 20 minuets more.
9. Leave calzone to cool down before slicing and serving.
10. Enjoy!

Nutritional Value: Calories 340; Fat 8g; Carbohydrates 6g; Protein 20g

Recipe 38: Chicken Wings with Thyme Chutney

Serving Size: 4

Cooking Time: 45 minutes

Ingredients:

- 12 chicken wings, cut in half
- 1 tablespoon turmeric
- 1 tablespoon cumin
- 3 tablespoon fresh ginger, grated
- 1 tablespoon cilantro, chopped
- 2 tablespoon paprika
- Salt and ground black pepper, to taste
- 3 tablespoon olive oil
- Juice of ½ lime
- 1 cup thyme leaves
- ¾ cup cilantro, chopped
- 1 tablespoon water
- 1 jalapeño pepper

Directions:

1. In a bowl, stir together 1 tablespoon ginger, cumin, paprika, salt, 2 tablespoon olive oil, black pepper, and turmeric. Place in the chicken wings pieces, toss to coat, and refrigerate for 20 minutes.
2. Heat the grill, place in the marinated wings, cook for 25 minutes, turning from time to time, remove and set to a serving plate.
3. Using a blender, combine thyme, remaining ginger, salt, jalapeno pepper, black pepper, lime juice, cilantro, remaining olive oil, and water, and blend well. Drizzle the chicken wings with the sauce to serve.

Nutritional Value: Calories 243; Fat 15g; Carbohydrates 3.5g; Protein 22g

Recipe 39: Coconut Pork and Celery

Serving Size: 4

Cooking Time: 8 hours

Ingredients:

- 2 shallots, chopped
- 2 pounds beef stew meat, cubed
- 1 tablespoon ghee, melted
- 1 cup tomato passata
- 2 jalapenos, minced
- 3 celery ribs, chopped
- 2 tablespoons coconut aminos
- A pinch of salt and black pepper
- A pinch of cayenne pepper
- 2 tablespoons cumin, ground
- 1 tablespoon oregano, chopped

Directions:

1. In your slow cooker, combine the meat with the shallots and the other ingredients, put the lid on and cook on Low for 8 hours.
2. Divide everything between plates and serve.

Nutritional Value: Calories 137; Fat 6g; Carbohydrates 5g; Protein 17g

Recipe 40: Garlic Pork and Zucchinis

Serving Size: 4

Cooking Time: 35 minutes

Ingredients:

- 2 tablespoons avocado oil
- 2 spring onions, chopped
- 1 pound pork stew meat, cubed
- 1 zucchini, cubed
- 3 garlic cloves, minced
- 1 cup tomato passata
- 1 cup cilantro, chopped
- A pinch of salt and black pepper
- 1 tablespoon oregano, chopped

Directions:

1. Heat up a large-sized pan with the oil over medium heat, add the garlic and the spring onions, stir and sauté for 2 minutes.
2. Add the meat and brown for approximately about 5 minutes more.
3. Add the rest of the prepared ingredients, toss, bring to a simmer and cook over medium heat for approximately about 20 minutes more.
4. Divide everything into bowls and serve.

Nutritional Value: Calories 274; Fat 12.1g; Carbohydrates 5.2g; Protein 34.9g

Recipe 41: Hazelnut and Cheese Stuffed Zucchinis

Serving Size: 4

Cooking Time: 35 minutes

Ingredients:

- 2 tablespoon olive oil
- 1 cup cauliflower rice
- ¼ cup vegetable broth
- 1 ¼ cup diced tomatoes
- 1 medium red onion, chopped
- ¼ cup pine nuts
- ¼ cup hazelnuts
- 4 tablespoon chopped cilantro
- 1 tablespoon balsamic vinegar
- 1 tablespoon smoked paprika
- 4 medium zucchinis, halved
- 1 cup grated Monterey Jack

Directions:

1. Preheat oven to 350 F. Pour cauli rice and broth in a pot and cook for 5 minutes. Fluff the cauli rice and allow cooling. Scoop the flesh out of the zucchini halves using a spoon and chop the pulp. Brush the inner parts of the vegetable with olive oil.
2. In a bowl, mix cauli rice, tomatoes, red onion, pine nuts, hazelnuts, cilantro, vinegar, paprika, and zucchini pulp. Spoon the mixture into the zucchini halves, drizzle with more olive oil, and sprinkle the cheese on top. Bake for 20 minutes until the cheese melts. Serve.

Nutritional Value: Calories 330; Fat 28g; Carbohydrates 5.2g; Protein 12g

Recipe 42: Lavender Lamb Chops

Serving Size: 4

Cooking Time: 25 minutes

Ingredients:

- 2 tablespoons rosemary, chopped
- 1 and ½ pounds lamb chops
- Salt and black pepper to the taste
- 1 tablespoon lavender, chopped
- 2 garlic cloves, minced
- 3 red oranges, cut in halves
- 2 small pieces of orange peel
- A drizzle of olive oil
- 1 teaspoon ghee

Directions:

1. In a large-sized bowl, mix lamb chops with salt, pepper, rosemary, lavender, garlic and orange peel, toss to coat and leave aside for a couple of hours.
2. Grease your kitchen grill with ghee, heat up over medium high heat, place lamb chops on it, cook for 3 minutes, flip, squeeze 1 orange half over them, cook for 3 minutes more, flip them again, cook them for 2 minutes and squeeze another orange half over them.
3. Place lamb chops on a plate and keep them warm for now..
4. Add remaining orange halves on preheated grill, cook them for 3 minutes, flip and cook them for another 3 minutes.
5. Divide lamb chops on plates, add orange halves on the side, drizzle some olive oil over them and serve.
6. Enjoy!

Nutritional Value: Calories 250; Fat 5g; Carbohydrates 5g; Protein 8g

Recipe 43: Meatballs and Pilaf

Serving Size: 4

Cooking Time: 30 minutes

Ingredients:

- 12 ozs. cauliflower florets
- Salt and black pepper to the taste
- 1 egg
- 1 lb. lamb, ground
- 1 teaspoon fennel seed
- 1 teaspoon paprika
- 1 teaspoon garlic powder
- 1 small yellow onion, chopped
- 2 garlic cloves, minced
- 2 tablespoons coconut oil
- 1 bunch mint, chopped
- 1 tablespoon lemon zest
- 4 ozs. goat cheese, crumbled

Directions:

1. Put cauliflower florets in your food processor, add salt and pulse well.
2. Grease a pan with some of the coconut oil, heat up over medium heat, add cauliflower rice, cook for 8 minutes, season with salt and pepper to the taste, take off heat and keep warm.
3. In a bowl, mix lamb with salt, pepper, egg, paprika, garlic powder and fennel seed and stir very well.
4. Shape 12 meatballs and place them on a plate for now.
5. Heat up a pan with the coconut oil over medium heat, add onion, stir and cook for 6 minutes.
6. Add garlic, stir and cook for 1 minute.
7. Add meatballs, cook them well on all sides and take off heat.
8. Divide cauliflower rice on plates, add meatballs and onion mix on top, sprinkle mint, lemon zest and goat cheese at the end and serve. Enjoy!

Nutritional Value: Calories 470; Fat 43g; Carbohydrates 4g; Protein 26g

Recipe 44: Mozzarella Chicken

Serving Size: 4

Cooking Time: 30 minutes

Ingredients:

- 1 pound chicken breast, skinless, boneless and cubed
- 1 tablespoon olive oil
- 2 shallots, chopped
- 1 cup tomatoes, cubed
- A pinch of salt and black pepper
- 1 cup mozzarella, shredded
- 1 tablespoon chives, chopped
- ¼ teaspoon sweet paprika

Directions:

1. Heat up a large-sized pan with the oil over medium high heat, add the shallots and sauté for 2 minutes.
2. Add the prepared chicken and brown for 5 minutes more.
3. Add the other ingredients except the cheese and toss.
4. Sprinkle the cheese on top, introduce the pan in the oven and bake at 390 degrees F for 15 minutes.
5. Divide everything between plates and serve.

Nutritional Value: Calories 223; Fat 8g; Carbohydrates 3g; Protein 26g

Recipe 45: Oregano Pork Chops

Serving Size: 4

Cooking Time: 36 minutes

Ingredients:

- 4 pork chops
- 1 tablespoon oregano, chopped
- 2 tablespoons olive oil
- 1 cup tomato passata
- A pinch of salt and black pepper
- 1 tablespoon cilantro, chopped
- 2 tablespoons lime juice

Directions:

1. Heat up a large-sized pan with the oil over medium high heat, add the pork chops and the oregano, and brown for 3 minutes on each side.
2. Add the rest of the prepared ingredients, toss, bring to a simmer and cook over medium heat for 30 minutes.
3. Divide the mix between plates and serve.

Nutritional Value: Calories 210; Fat 10g; Carbohydrates 6g; Protein 19g

Recipe 46: Parsley Pork and Beef Meatballs

Serving Size: 4

Cooking Time: 12 minutes

Ingredients:

- 1 pound beef meat, ground
- ½ pound pork stew meat, ground
- 2 eggs, whisked
- ¼ cup coconut flour
- 1 cup parsley, minced
- 2 garlic cloves, minced
- 2 tablespoons ghee, melted
- A pinch of salt and black pepper

Directions:

1. In a large-sized bowl, combine the beef and pork meat with the other ingredients except the ghee, stir well and shape medium meatballs out of this mix.
2. Heat up a large-sized pan with the ghee over medium heat, add the meatballs, cook them for 6 minutes on each side, divide between plates and serve.

Nutritional Value: Calories 435; Fat 23g; Carbohydrates 6g; Protein 32g

Recipe 47: Portobello Mushroom with Sausage and Cheese

Serving Size: 2

Cooking Time: 20 minutes

Ingredients:

- 2 Portobello mushroom caps2 oz sausage
- 1 tablespoon melted butter, unsalted
- 2 tablespoon grated parmesan cheese

Seasoning:
- 1/8 teaspoon garlic powder
- 1/8 teaspoon red chili powder
- ¼ teaspoon salt
- 2 teaspoon avocado oil

Directions:

1. Turn on the oven, then set it to 425 degrees F and let it preheat.
2. Meanwhile, remove the stems from mushroom caps, chop them and then brush the caps with butter inside-out.
3. Take a frying pan, place it over medium heat, add oil and when hot, add sausage, crumble it, sprinkle with garlic powder and then cook for 5 minutes until cooked.
4. Stir in mushroom stems, season with salt and black pepper, continue cooking for 3 minutes until cooked and then remove the pan from heat.
5. Distribute sausage-mushroom mixture into mushroom caps, sprinkle cheese, and red chili powder on top and then bake for 10 t0 12 minutes until mushroom caps have turned tender and cooked. Serve.

Nutritional Value: Calories 310; Fat 26g; Carbohydrates 6.6g; Protein 10.7g

Recipe 48: Rosemary Pork

Serving Size: 4

Cooking Time: 30 minutes

Ingredients:

- 1 lb. pork stew meat, roughly cubed
- 1 tablespoon olive oil
- 2 shallots, chopped
- 1 tablespoon rosemary, chopped
- 1 cup beef stock
- 1 teaspoon sweet paprika
- A pinch of salt and black pepper

Directions:

1. Heat up a pan with the oil over medium heat, add the shallots and the meat and brown for 5 minutes.
2. Add the rosemary and the other ingredients, toss, bring to a simmer and cook over medium heat for 25 minutes more.
3. Divide the mix between plates and serve.

Nutritional Value: Calories 279; Fat 14.8g; Carbohydrates 1.3g; Protein 34g

Recipe 49: Sage Beef

Serving Size: 4

Cooking Time: 35 minutes

Ingredients:

- 2 garlic cloves, minced
- 1 pound beef stew meat, cubed
- 2 tablespoons ghee, melted
- 2 shallots, chopped
- 1 celery stalks, chopped
- ½ cup beef stock
- A pinch of salt and black pepper
- 1 teaspoon cumin, ground
- 1 tablespoon sage, chopped

Directions:

1. Heat up a large-sized pan with the oil over medium high heat, add the garlic and the shallots and sauté for 5 minutes.
2. Add the meat and brown for approximately about 5 minutes more.
3. Add the rest of the prepared ingredients, toss, bring to a simmer and cook over medium heat for 25 minutes.

Nutritional Value: Calories 222; Fat 10g; Carbohydrates 8g; Protein 21g

Recipe 50: Sausage with Tomatoes and Cheese

Serving Size: 4

Cooking Time: 30 minutes

Ingredients:

- 2 ounces coconut oil, melted
- 2 pounds Italian pork sausage, chopped
- 1 onion, sliced
- 4 sun dried tomatoes, thinly sliced
- Salt and black pepper to the taste
- ½ pound gouda cheese, grated
- 3 yellow bell peppers, chopped
- 3 orange bell peppers, chopped
- A pinch of red pepper flakes
- A handful parsley, thinly sliced

Directions:

1. Heat up a large-sized pan with the oil over medium high heat, add sausage slices, stir, cook for 3 minutes on each side, transfer to a plate and leave aside for now.
2. Heat up the large-sized pan again over medium heat, add onion, yellow and orange bell peppers and tomatoes, stir and cook for 5 minutes.
3. Add the prepared pepper flakes, salt and pepper, stir well, cook for 1 minute and take off heat.
4. Arrange sausage slices into a baking dish, add bell peppers mix on top, add parsley and gouda as well, introduce in the oven at 350 degrees F and bake for 15 minutes.
5. Divide on plates and serve hot.
6. Enjoy!

Nutritional Value: Calories 200; Fat 5g; Carbohydrates 6g; Protein 14g

Recipe 51: Seared Scallops and Roasted Grapes

Serving Size: 4

Cooking Time: 10 minutes

Ingredients:

- 1 pound scallops
- 3 tablespoons olive oil
- 1 shallot, chopped
- 3 garlic cloves, minced
- 2 cups spinach
- 1 cup chicken stock
- 1 romanesco lettuce head
- 1 and ½ cups red grapes, cut in halves
- ¼ cup walnuts, toasted and chopped
- 1 tablespoon ghee
- Salt and black pepper to the taste

Directions:

2. Put romanesco in your food processor, blend and transfer to a bowl.
3. Heat up a large-sized pan with 2 tablespoons oil over medium high heat, add shallot and garlic, stir and cook for 1 minute.
4. Add romanesco, spinach and 1 cup stock, stir, cook for 3 minutes, blend using an immersion blender and take off heat.
5. Heat up another pan with 1 tablespoon oil and the ghee over medium high heat, add scallops, season with salt and pepper, cook for 2 minutes, flip and sear for 1 minute more.
6. Divide romanesco mix on plates, add scallops on the side, top with walnuts and grapes and serve.
7. Enjoy!

Nutritional Value: Calories 300; Fat 12g; Carbohydrates 6g; Protein 20g

Recipe 52: Spicy Chicken Leg Quarters

Serving Size: 3

Cooking Time: 53 minutes

Ingredients:

- 3 10-11 ozs. grass-fed bone-in, skin-on chicken leg quarters
- ½ cup mayonnaise
- 1 teaspoon paprika
- ½ teaspoon garlic powder
- Salt and ground white pepper, as required

Directions:

1. Preheat the oven to 350 degrees. Generously, grease a baking dish.
2. Add the mayonnaise in a shallow bowl.
3. Place the paprika, garlic powder, salt and white pepper in a small bowl and mix well.
4. Coat each chicken quarter with mayonnaise and then, sprinkle evenly with the spice mixture.
5. Arrange the chicken quarters onto prepared baking sheet in a single layer.
6. Bake for about 45 minutes.
7. Now, increase the temperature of oven to 400 degrees F and bake for about 5-8 more minutes.
8. Remove from oven and place the chicken quarters onto a platter.
9. With a piece of foil, cover each chicken quarter loosely for about 5-10 minutes before serving.
10. Serve.

Nutritional Value: Calories 725; Fat 0.5g; Carbohydrates 59.7g; Protein 48.3g

Recipe 53: Steak with Blueberry Sauce

Serving Size: 4

Cooking Time: 20 minutes

Ingredients:

For Sauce:
- 2 tablespoons butter
- 2 tablespoons yellow onion, chopped
- 2 garlic cloves, minced
- 1 teaspoon fresh thyme, finely chopped
- 1 1/3 cups homemade beef broth
- 2 tablespoons fresh lemon juice
- ¾ cup fresh blueberries

For Steak:
- 2 tablespoons butter
- 4 6-ounces grass-fed flank steaks
- Salt and ground black pepper, as required

Directions:

1. For sauce: in a pan, melt butter over medium heat and sauté the onion for about 2-3 minutes. Add the garlic, and thyme and sauté for about 1 minute.
2. Stir in the broth and bring to a gentle simmer.
3. Adjust the heat to low and cook for about 10 minutes.
4. Meanwhile, for the steak: season it with salt and black pepper.
5. In a skillet, melt the butter over medium-high heat and cook steaks for about 3-4 minutes per side. With a slotted spoon, transfer the steak onto serving plates.
6. Add sauce in the skillet and stir to scrape up brown bits from the bottom.
7. Stir in the lemon juice, blueberries, salt, and black pepper and cook for about 1-2 minutes.
8. Remove from heat and place blueberry sauce over the steaks.
9. Serve immediately.

Nutritional Value: Calories 467; Fat 3.3g; Carbohydrates 4.6g; Protein 49.5g

Recipe 54: Tangy Chicken Drumsticks

Serving Size: 5

Cooking Time: 1 hour 15 minutes

Ingredients:

- 2 tablespoons olive oil
- 2 lbs. chicken drumsticks, boneless, skinless
- Sea salt and ground black pepper, to taste
- 2 garlic cloves, minced
- 1/2 cup tomato paste
- 1/2 cup chicken broth
- 4 tablespoons rice vinegar
- 2 scallions, chopped

Directions:

1. Start by preheating the oven to 330 degrees F. Brush the sides and bottom of a baking pan with olive oil.
2. Arrange the chicken drumsticks in the baking pan. Add the salt, black pepper, garlic, tomato paste, chicken broth, and rice vinegar to the pan.
3. Bake for approximately about 1 hour 10 minutes or until everything is heated through.
4. Garnish with scallions and serve. Bon appétit!

Nutritional Value: Calories 352; Fat 22.1g; Carbohydrates 2g; Protein 33.3g

Recipe 55: Tender Chicken Thighs

Serving Size: 4

Cooking Time: 45 minutes

Ingredients:

- 3 tablespoons ghee
- 8 ounces mushrooms, sliced
- 2 tablespoons gruyere cheese, grated
- Salt and black pepper to the taste
- 2 garlic cloves, minced
- 6 chicken thighs, skin and bone-in

Directions:

1. Heat up a large-sized pan with 1 tablespoon ghee over medium heat, add chicken thighs, season with salt and pepper, cook for 3 minutes on each side and arrange them into a baking dish.
2. Heat up the pan again with the rest of the ghee over medium heat, add garlic, stir and cook for 1 minute.
3. Add mushrooms and stir well.
4. Add salt and pepper, stir and cook for 10 minutes.
5. Spoon these over chicken, sprinkle cheese, introduce in the oven at 350 degrees F and bake for 30 minutes.
6. Turn oven to broiler and broil everything for a couple more minutes.
7. Divide on plates and serve.
8. Enjoy!

Nutritional Value: Calories 340; Fat 31g; Carbohydrates 5g; Protein 64g

Recipe 56: Thyme Beef and Leeks

Serving Size: 4

Cooking Time: 35 minutes

Ingredients:

- 2 pounds beef stew meat, cubed
- 2 tablespoons ghee, melted
- A pinch of salt and black pepper
- 2 leeks, sliced
- 1 cup beef stock
- 3 garlic cloves, minced
- 1 teaspoon oregano, dried
- 1 tablespoon thyme, chopped

Directions:

1. Heat up a large-sized pan with the ghee over medium high heat, add the leeks and garlic and sauté for 5 minutes.
2. Add the meat and brown for approximately about 5 minutes more.
3. Add the stock and the rest of the ingredients, bring to a simmer and cook over medium heat for 25 minutes more.
4. Divide everything into bowls and serve.

Nutritional Value: Calories 260; Fat 7g; Carbohydrates 4g; Protein 10g

Recipe 57: Trout and Endives

Serving Size: 2

Cooking Time: 15 minutes

Ingredients:

- 4 trout fillets
- 2 endives, shredded
- ½ cup shallots, chopped
- 2 tablespoons olive oil
- 1 teaspoon rosemary, dried
- ¼ cup chicken stock
- A pinch of salt and black pepper
- 2 tablespoons chives, chopped

Directions:

1. Heat up a large-sized pan with the oil over medium heat, add the shallots and the endives, toss and cook for 2 minutes.
2. Add the fish and cook it for 2 minutes on each side.
3. Add the rest of the prepared ingredients, cook for 8-9 minutes more, divide between plates and serve.

Nutritional Value: Calories 200; Fat 5g; Carbohydrates 2g; Protein 7g

Recipe 58: Veal Parmesan

Serving Size: 6

Cooking Time: 1 hour 10 minutes

Ingredients:

- 8 veal cutlets
- 2/3 cup parmesan, grated
- 8 provolone cheese slices
- Salt and black pepper to the taste
- 5 cups tomato sauce
- A pinch of garlic salt
- Cooking spray
- 2 tablespoons ghee
- 2 tablespoons coconut oil, melted
- 1 teaspoon Italian seasoning

Directions:

1. Season veal cutlets with salt, pepper and garlic salt an drub,
2. Heat up a pan with the ghee and the oil over medium high heat, add veal and cook until they brown on all sides.
3. Spread half of the tomato sauce on the bottom of a baking dish which you've greased with some cooking spray.
4. Add veal cutlets, then sprinkle Italian seasoning and spread the rest of the sauce.
5. Cover dish, introduce in the oven at 350 degrees F and bake for 40 minutes.
6. Uncover dish, spread provolone cheese and sprinkle parmesan, introduce in the oven again and bake for 15 minutes more.
7. Divide on plates and serve. Enjoy!

Nutritional Value: Calories 362; Fat 21g; Carbohydrates 6g; Protein 26g

Recipe 59: White Wine Lamb Chops

Serving Size: 6

Cooking Time: 1 hour 10 minutes

Ingredients:

- 6 lamb chops
- 1 tablespoon sage
- 1 teaspoon thyme
- 1 onion, sliced
- 3 garlic cloves, minced
- 2 tablespoon olive oil
- ½ cup white wine
- Salt and black pepper, to taste

Directions:

1. Heat the olive oil in a pan. Add onion and garlic and cook for 3 minutes, until soft. Rub the sage and thyme over the lamb chops. Cook the lamb for about 3 minutes per side. Set aside.
2. Pour the white wine and 1 cup of water into the pan, bring the mixture to a boil. Cook until the liquid is reduced by half. Add the chops in the pan, reduce the heat, and let simmer for 1 hour.

Nutritional Value: Calories 397; Fat 30g; Carbohydrates 4.3g; Protein 16g

Recipe 60: Zucchini Quiche with Pancetta

Serving Size: 3

Cooking Time: 25 minutes

Ingredients:

- 3 medium zucchinis, diced
- 6 pancetta slices
- 3 egg
- 3 tablespoon olive oil
- 1 yellow onion, chopped
- 1 tablespoon cilantro, chopped

Directions:

1. Place pancetta in a skillet and cook for 5 minutes, until crispy; set aside.
2. Warm olive oil and stir-fry onion for 3 minutes. Add zucchini, and cook for 10 more minutes.
3. Transfer to a plate and season with salt. Crack the egg into the same skillet and fry over medium heat.
4. Top the zucchini mixture with pancetta slices and a fried egg.

Nutritional Value: Calories 423; Fat 35g; Carbohydrates 6.6g; Protein 17g

Chapter 3:   Dinner Recipes

Recipe 61: Bacon Wrapped Sausages

Serving Size: 4

Cooking Time: 30 minutes

Ingredients:

- 8 bacon strips
- 8 sausages
- 16 pepper jack cheese slices
- Salt and black pepper to the taste
- A pinch of garlic powder
- ½ teaspoon sweet paprika
- 1 pinch of onion powder

Directions:

1. Heat up your kitchen grill over medium heat, add sausages, cook for a few minutes on each side, transfer to a plate and leave them aside for a few minutes to cool down.
2. Cut a slit in the middle of each sausage to create pockets, stuff each with 2 cheese slices and season with salt, pepper, paprika, onion and garlic powder.
3. Wrap each stuffed sausage in a bacon strip, secure with toothpicks, place on a lined baking sheet, introduce in the oven at 400 degrees F and bake for 15 minutes.
4. Serve hot for lunch!
5. Enjoy!

Nutritional Value: Calories 500; Fat 37g; Carbohydrates 4g; Protein 40g

Recipe 62: Baked Calamari and Shrimp

Serving Size: 2

Cooking Time: 20 minutes

Ingredients:

- 8 ounces calamari, cut in medium rings
- 7 ounces shrimp, peeled and deveined
- 1 eggs
- 3 tablespoons coconut flour
- 1 tablespoon coconut oil
- 2 tablespoons avocado, chopped
- 1 teaspoon tomato paste
- 1 tablespoon mayonnaise
- A splash of Worcestershire sauce
- 1 teaspoon lemon juice
- 2 lemon slices
- Salt and black pepper to the taste
- ½ teaspoon turmeric

Directions:

1. In a bowl, whisk egg with coconut oil.
2. Add calamari rings and shrimp and toss to coat.
3. In another bowl, mix flour with salt, pepper and turmeric and stir.
4. Dredge calamari and shrimp in this mix, place everything on a lined baking sheet, introduce in the oven at 400 degrees F and bake for 10 minutes.
5. Flip calamari and shrimp and bake for 10 minutes more.
6. Meanwhile, in a bowl, mix avocado with mayo and tomato paste and mash using a fork.
7. Add Worcestershire sauce, lemon juice, salt and pepper and stir well.
8. Divide baked calamari and shrimp on plates and serve with the sauce and lemon juice on the side. Enjoy!

Nutritional Value: Calories 368; Fat 23g; Carbohydrates 10g; Protein 34g

Recipe 63: Baked Sausage and Kale

Serving Size: 4

Cooking Time: 30 minutes

Ingredients:

- 1 cup yellow onion, chopped
- 1 and ½ pound Italian pork sausage, sliced
- ½ cup red bell pepper, chopped
- Salt and black pepper to the taste
- 5 pounds kale, chopped
- 1 teaspoon garlic, minced
- ¼ cup red hot chili pepper, chopped
- 1 cup water

Directions:

1. Heat up a large-sized pan over medium high heat, add sausage, stir, reduce heat to medium and cook for 10 minutes.
2. Add onions, stir and cook for approximately about 3-4 minutes more.
3. Add bell pepper and garlic, stir and cook for 1 minute.
4. Add kale, chili pepper, salt, pepper and water, stir and cook for 10 minutes more.
5. Divide on plates and serve.
6. Enjoy!

Nutritional Value: Calories 150; Fat 4g; Carbohydrates 2g; Protein 12g

Recipe 64: Barbecued Pork Chops

Serving Size: 2

Cooking Time: 15 minutes

Ingredients:

- 2 pork loin chops, boneless
- ½ cup BBQ sauce, sugar-free
- Salt and black pepper to taste
- 1 tablespoon erythritol
- ½ teaspoon ginger powder
- ½ teaspoon onion powder
- ½ teaspoon garlic powder
- 1 teaspoon red pepper flakes
- 2 thyme sprigs, chopped

Directions:

1. Mix black pepper, salt, ginger powder, onion powder, garlic powder, and red pepper flakes, and rub the pork chops on all sides. Preheat the grill to 4500 F and cook the meat for 2 minutes per side.
2. Reduce the heat and brush the BBQ sauce on the meat, cover, and grill for another 5 minutes.
3. Open the lid, turn the meat and brush again with barbecue sauce. Continue cooking covered for 5 minutes. Remove the meat to a serving platter and serve sprinkled with thyme.

Nutritional Value: Calories 412; Fat 34.6g; Carbohydrates 1.1g; Protein 34.1g

Recipe 65: Bell Peppers and Sausage

Serving Size: 4

Cooking Time: 10 minutes

Ingredients:

- ¾-cup tomato spaghetti sauce
- 5-oz. mozzarella cheese, grated.
- 1 large red pepper, thickly sliced.
- 6-oz. onion, chopped.
- 1¼-lbs. Italian sausages.
- 2-tablespoon olive oil
- 1 large green bell pepper, chunked.
- 2 cloves garlic, finely chopped

Directions:

1. Brown the sausages in a skillet over a medium heat. When the sausages are partially cooked add in the peppers, onion and garlic
2. Continue to actually cook until the sausages are done and the vegetables are still crisp. Take the sausages out of the skillet and slice into chunky bite sized pieces. Return to the pan
3. Stir in the spaghetti sauce and cover. Simmer for approximately about 5 to 8 minutes until all is piping hot. Sprinkle with the cheese and serve.

Nutritional Value: Calories 434; Fat 60g; Carbohydrates 18g; Protein 21.6g

Recipe 66: Cashew Chicken Curry

Serving Size: 4

Cooking Time: 25 minutes

Ingredients:

- 1 cups Cauliflower
- 2 large fresh tomatoes
- 1 medium red onion
- 2 cups Cucumber
- 2 tablespoon Coconut oil
- 1 lb. Breasts of chicken
- 1 large Egg white
- For the Garnish:
- Freshly chopped fresh mint
- Minced fresh cilantro
- Food processor & Rimmed baking sheet

Directions:

1. Chop the cauliflower into florets and quarter the tomatoes. Roughly chop the onion and thinly slice the cucumber into halves. Take off the skin and bones from the chicken.
2. Heat the oven to 425° Fahrenheit.
3. Toss the quartered tomatoes, cauliflower florets, and onion into a mixing container. Melt the coconut oil and sprinkle using 1.5 teaspoons of curry powder. Mix until well.
4. Prepare on a baking sheet in one layer. Dust with pepper and salt to your liking. Add the rest of the curry powder and cashews into a food processor. Pulse leaving a few chunks for texture.
5. Pat to remove the moisture from the chicken breasts using a paper towel.
6. Put the egg white and cashews into two shallow plates.
7. Dredge the chicken through the egg white. Shake off any excess and press into the cashews.
8. Flip and lightly press the other side into the cashews.
9. Put the chicken breast onto a small cooling rack that fits on your sheet pan (one with legs is preferred, so it sits over the veggies).
10. Continue the process with the remaining chicken. Place the cooling rack over a sheet pan (over the top of the veggies).
11. Bake the chicken to reach an internal temperature of 165° Fahrenheit (14-15 min.). Once it's done, toss the fresh cucumbers onto the pan.
12. Garnish with mint and cilantro.

Nutritional Value: Calories 364; Fat 18g; Carbohydrates 14g; Protein 34g

Recipe 67: Cheesy Ham with Cauliflower Mash

Serving Size: 8

Cooking Time: 50 minutes

Ingredients:

- 1 large head cauliflower, cut into pieces.
- ½-cup sour cream
- 2-oz. green onion, chopped.
- 8-oz. sharp cheddar cheese.
- 14-oz. ham, diced
- 8-oz. cream cheese.
- Salt and pepper to taste
- Paprika to garnish

Directions:

1. Pre heat your oven to the 350 degree °F. Have ready a greased 3-quart casserole with a lid. Cook the cauliflower until tender and drain very well
2. Place the cauliflower into the casserole. In a bowl mix together the cream cheese, sour cream, onion, seasoning, ham and cheddar
3. Add to the cauliflower and sprinkle with paprika. Cover and bake for 35 minutes. Uncover and continue baking for another 15 minutes to brown the top.

Nutritional Value: Calories 353; Fat 26.7g; Carbohydrates 9.7g; Protein 20.1g

Recipe 68: Chicken and Garlic Green Beans

Serving Size: 4

Cooking Time: 30 minutes

Ingredients:

- 1 pound chicken breast, skinless and boneless and roughly cubed
- 2 tablespoons avocado oil
- 2 shallots, chopped
- ½ pound green beans, trimmed and halved
- 4 garlic cloves, mined
- 1 cup chicken stock
- ½ cup tomato passata
- 1 tablespoon cilantro, chopped
- A pinch of salt and black pepper

Directions:

1. Heat up a large-sized pan with the oil over medium heat, add the shallots and the meat and brown for 5 minutes.
2. Add the garlic and the green beans, and cook for 5 minutes more.
3. Add the rest of the ingredients, toss gently, bring to a simmer and cook over medium heat for 20 minutes more.
4. Divide between plates and serve.

Nutritional Value: Calories 240; Fat 4g; Carbohydrates 6g; Protein 20g

Recipe 69: Chicken and Mushrooms

Serving Size: 4

Cooking Time: 30 minutes

Ingredients:

- 1 pound chicken breast, skinless, boneless and cubed
- 2 cups baby bella mushrooms, sliced
- 2 tablespoons olive oil
- 1 red onion, chopped
- 1 red bell pepper, chopped
- 2 garlic cloves, minced
- A pinch of salt and black pepper
- ½ cup chicken stock
- 1 tablespoon balsamic vinegar
- 1 tablespoon parsley, chopped

Directions:

1. Heat up a large-sized pan with the oil over medium heat, add the onion and the mushrooms, stir and cook for 5 minutes.
2. Add the chicken, toss and brown for 5 minutes more.
3. Add the rest of the prepared ingredients, toss, bring to a simmer and cook over medium heat for 20 minutes.
4. Divide everything between plates and serve.

Nutritional Value: Calories 340; Fat 33g; Carbohydrates 4g; Protein 20g

Recipe 70: Chicken Pasta

Serving Size: 4

Cooking Time: 30 minutes

Ingredients:

- 2 tablespoons ghee
- 1 teaspoon garlic, minced
- 1 pound chicken cutlets
- 1 teaspoon Cajun seasoning
- ¼ cup scallions, chopped
- ½ cup tomatoes, chopped
- ½ cup chicken stock
- ¼ cup whipping cream
- ½ cup cheddar cheese, grated
- 1 ounce cream cheese
- ¼ cup cilantro, chopped
- Salt and black pepper to the taste

For the pasta:
- 4 ounces cream cheese
- 8 eggs
- Salt and black pepper to the taste
- A pinch of garlic powder

Directions:

1. Heat up a large-sized pan with 1 tablespoon ghee over medium heat, add chicken cutlets, season with some of the Cajun seasoning, cook for 2 minutes on each side and transfer to a plate.
2. Heat up the pan with the rest of the ghee over medium heat, add garlic, stir and cook for 2 minutes.
3. Add tomatoes, stir and cook for 2 minutes more.
4. Add stock and the rest of the Cajun seasoning, stir and cook for 5 minutes.
5. Add whipping cream, cheddar cheese, 1 ounce cream cheese, salt, pepper, scallions and cilantro, stir well, cook for 2 minutes more and take off heat.
6. Meanwhile, in your blender, mix 4 ounces cream cheese with eggs, salt, pepper and garlic powder and pulse well.
7. Pour this into a lined baking sheet, leave aside for 5 minutes and then bake in the oven at 325 degrees F for 10 minutes.
8. Leave pasta sheet to cool down, transfer to a cutting board, roll and cut into medium slices.
9. Divide pasta on plates, top with chicken mix and serve.
10. Enjoy!

Nutritional Value: Calories 345; Fat 34g; Carbohydrates 4g; Protein 39g

Recipe 71: Cod with Bok Choy

Serving Size: 2

Cooking Time: 20 minutes

Ingredients:

- ½ lb. baby bok choy, halved lengthwise.
- ¼ cup {½ stick} butter, thinly sliced.
- 2 {8-ounce} cod fillets.
- 1 tablespoon minced garlic
- ¼ teaspoon freshly ground black pepper.
- ¼ teaspoon salt

Directions:

1. Preheat your oven to 400-Degrees F. Make a large pouch from aluminum foil and place the cod inside. Top with slices of butter and the garlic, evenly divided
2. Tuck the bok choy around the fillets. Season with the pepper and salt. Close the pouch with the two ends of the foil meeting at the top, so the butter remains in the pouch.
3. Place the sealed pouches in a baking dish. Put the dish in the prepared preheated oven and bake for 15 to 20 minutes, depending on the thickness of the fillets
4. Remove the dish from the oven and check the fillets for doneness. Serve immediately.

Nutritional Value: Calories 317; Fat 23.8g; Carbohydrates 4g; Protein 22.6g

Recipe 72: Crusted Lamb Chops

Serving Size: 4

Cooking Time: 15 minutes

Ingredients:

- 2 lamb racks, cut into chops
- Salt and black pepper to the taste
- 3 tablespoons paprika
- ¾ cup cumin powder
- 1 teaspoon chili powder

Directions:

1. In a bowl, mix paprika with cumin, chili, salt and pepper and stir.
2. Add lamb chops and rub them well.
3. Heat up your grill over medium temperature, add lamb chops, cook for 5 minutes, flip and cook for 5 minutes more.
4. Flip them again, cook for 2 minutes and then for 2 minutes more on the other side again.
5. Enjoy!

Nutritional Value: Calories 200; Fat 5g; Carbohydrates 4g; Protein 8g

Recipe 73: Cuban Steak with Onions

Serving Size: 4

Cooking Time: 10 minutes

Ingredients:

- 1 lb. sirloin steak
- 2 cloves garlic, peeled and chopped
- 1 teaspoon adobo seasoning
- ¼ cup vinegar
- 3 large red onions, peeled and sliced

Directions:

1. In a large mixing bowl, mix the garlic, adobo seasoning, and vinegar together.
2. Add the steak to the seasoning mix and marinate for 30 minutes.
3. While the steak is marinating, sauté the onions in a large skillet over medium heat with coconut oil until translucent. Set aside once cooked.
4. In the same sauté pan that you used for the onions and cook the steak until desired doneness is reached. Serve with the onions.

Nutritional Value: Calories 259; Fat 12g; Carbohydrates 12g; Protein 24g

Recipe 74: Lamb with Fennel and Figs

Serving Size: 4

Cooking Time: 40 minutes

Ingredients:

- 12 ounces lamb racks
- 2 fennel bulbs, sliced
- Salt and black pepper to the taste
- 2 tablespoons olive oil
- 4 figs, cut in halves
- 1/8 cup apple cider vinegar
- 1 tablespoon swerve

Directions:

1. In a bowl, mix fennel with figs, vinegar, swerve and oil, toss to coat well and transfer to a baking dish.
2. Season with prepared salt and pepper, introduce in the oven at 400 degrees F and bake for 15 minutes.
3. Season lamb with salt and pepper, place into a heated pan over medium high heat and cook for a couple of minutes.
4. Add lamb to the baking dish with the fennel and figs, introduce in the oven and bake for 20 minutes more.
5. Divide everything on plates and serve.
6. Enjoy!

Nutritional Value: Calories 230; Fat 3g; Carbohydrates 5g; Protein 10g

Recipe 75: Lean and Green Broccoli Alfredo

Serving Size: 5

Cooking Time: 10 minutes

Ingredients:

- 2 heads of broccoli, cut into florets
- 2 tablespoons lemon juice, freshly squeezed
- ½ cup cashew, soaked for 2 hours in water then drained
- 2 tablespoons white miso, low sodium
- 2 teaspoon Dijon mustard
- Freshly cracked black pepper

Directions:

1. Boil water in a pot using a medium flame. Blanch the broccoli for 2 minutes, then place it in a bowl of iced water. Drain.
2. In a food processor, place the remaining ingredients and pulse until smooth.
3. Pour the alfredo sauce over the broccoli. Toss to coat with the sauce.

Nutritional Value: Calories 359; Fat 8.4g; Carbohydrates 50.2g; Protein 10.6g

Recipe 76: Nutmeg Beef Bowls

Serving Size: 4

Cooking Time: 30 minutes

Ingredients:

- 2 pounds beef stew meat, cubed
- 1 tablespoon ghee, melted
- 1 teaspoon nutmeg, ground
- 1 cup beef stock
- A pinch of salt and black pepper
- 2 tablespoons chives, chopped
- 1 cup tomato passata
- ¼ teaspoon garlic powder

Directions:

1. Heat up a large-sized pan with the ghee over medium heat, add the meat and brown for 5 minutes.
2. Add the rest of the prepared ingredients, bring to a simmer and cook over medium heat for 25 minutes more.
3. Divide everything into bowls and serve.

Nutritional Value: Calories 275; Fat 7g; Carbohydrates 4g; Protein 10g

Recipe 77: Onions with Spicy Sausage

Serving Size: 8

Cooking Time: 40 minutes

Ingredients:

- 1-cup mature cheddar cheese, grated.
- ½-cup parmesan cheese, grated.
- 8-oz. button mushrooms, sliced.
- 9 extra-large fresh eggs.
- 1-lb. hot breakfast sausage, skinned.
- 1 medium brown onion, diced.
- 2-tablespoon butter
- 2½-tablespoon garlic, finely chopped.
- 3-tablespoon tomato paste
- 1-tablespoon chili sauce
- Salt and pepper

Directions:

1. Pre heat your oven to the 350 degree °F. Have ready a large baking dish. Caramelize the onions and garlic in the butter, in a large skillet. Season with pepper and salt. About 25 minutes over a low heat.
2. In another skillet brown the sausage meat. When the sausage is nearly cooked. Add the mushrooms, tomato paste and chili sauce
3. Crack the eggs into a large bowl and beat well. Add the cheeses to the beaten eggs. Place the meat mixture into the baking dish and pour the egg mixture evenly over the top
4. With the back of a spoon make indentations into the sausage to form 'puddles' of egg. Place in the prepared oven and bake for approximately about 35 to 40 minutes until golden brown.

Nutritional Value: Calories 404; Fat 31.7g; Carbohydrates 4.9g; Protein 24.9g

Recipe 78: Orange Chili Lobster

Serving Size: 4

Cooking Time: 20 minutes

Ingredients:

- 4 lobster tails, split down the back of the shell.
- 2-tablespoon butter.
- ½-teaspoon Splenda
- 1-teaspoon lemon juice.
- 1½-teaspoon chili garlic paste.
- ¼-teaspoon orange extract

Directions:

1. Your lobster tails should have their shells split along the back. Put them on a broiler rack. Melt the butter, and stir in everything else.
2. Baste the lobster tails with this mixture, being sure to get some down into the shell. Place tails 5" to 6" under broiler, set on high
3. Broil for 7 to 8 minutes, basting every couple of minutes with the butter mixture, ending the basting about 2 minutes before the end of cooking time. Serve.

Nutritional Value: Calories 308; Fat 8g; Carbohydrates 2g; Protein 53g

Recipe 79: Orange Glazed Salmon

Serving Size: 2

Cooking Time: 10 minutes

Ingredients:

- 2 lemons, sliced
- 1 pound wild salmon, skinless and cubed
- ¼ cup balsamic vinegar
- ¼ cup red orange juice
- 1 teaspoon coconut oil
- 1/3 cup orange marmalade, no sugar added

Directions:

1. Heat up a pot over medium heat, add vinegar, orange juice and marmalade, stir well, bring to a simmer for 1 minute, reduce temperature, cook until it thickens a bit and take off heat.
2. Arrange salmon and lemon slices on skewers and brush them on one side with the orange glaze.
3. Brush your kitchen grill with coconut oil and heat up over medium heat.
4. Place salmon kebabs on grill with glazed side down and cook for 4 minutes.
5. Flip kebabs, brush them with the rest of the orange glaze and cook for 4 minutes more.
6. Serve right away.
7. Enjoy!

Nutritional Value: Calories 160; Fat 3g; Carbohydrates 1g; Protein 8g

Recipe 80: Oven-Baked Sole Fillets

Serving Size: 4

Cooking Time: 20 minutes

Ingredients:

- 2 tablespoons olive oil
- 1/2 tablespoon Dijon mustard
- 1 teaspoon garlic paste
- 1/2 tablespoon fresh ginger, minced
- 1/2 teaspoon porcini powder
- Salt and ground black pepper, to taste
- 1/2 teaspoon paprika
- 4 sole fillets
- 1/4 cup fresh parsley, chopped

Directions:

1. Combine the oil, Dijon mustard, garlic paste, ginger, porcini powder, salt, black pepper, and paprika.
2. Rub this mixture all over sole fillets. Place the sole fillets in a lightly oiled baking pan.
3. Bake in the preheated oven at 400 degrees F for about 20 minutes.

Nutritional Value: Calories 195; Fat 8.2g; Carbohydrates 0.5g; Protein 28.7g

Recipe 81: Pork Schnitzel

Serving Size: 4

Cooking Time: 20 minutes

Ingredients:

- 2-oz. flax seed, ground.
- 1-oz. sesame seed, ground.
- ½-cup milk.
- 1½-lbs. boneless pork loin slices.
- 2-tablespoon olive oil
- 2-tablespoon butter
- 2 eggs
- Pinch pepper and salt

Directions:

1. Pound each pork slice until really thin. Mix the flaxseed, sesame, pepper and salt and spread out on a large plate
2. Beat the prepared egg and milk together and season to taste. Coat the pork slices with egg and milk and then put them in the dry mixture. Make sure they are evenly coated.
3. Place on a large plate covered with baking paper and rest in the fridge for 15 minutes. Heat the prepared oil and butter in a large non-stick skillet over a medium high heat
4. Lay the pork slices in the oil and fry carefully until cooked and golden brown. About 4 minutes for each side.
5. Drain on paper towel and serve whilst still hot. Serve with a crunchy green salad and lemon slices if liked.

Nutritional Value: Calories 486; Fat 30.3g; Carbohydrates 8.4g; Protein 34.7g

Recipe 82: Pork with Mayonnaise

Serving Size: 4

Cooking Time: 40 minutes

Ingredients:

- 1 small onion, thinly sliced.
- ½ chicken stock cube, dissolved in ¾-cup of boiling water
- 2-tablespoon fresh rosemary, finely chopped.
- 1-lb. boneless pork steaks, about ½ inch thick.
- 1-teaspoon onion powder
- 7-tablespoon mayonnaise
- 1-tablespoon corn flour dissolved in 1 tablespoon of cold water.
- 2-tablespoon of freshly chopped parsley.
- 2-tablespoon olive oil
- Pinch ground black pepper and cayenne pepper

Directions:

1. Pre heat your oven to the 350 degree °F. Flatten the pork steaks with a mallet and sprinkle with onion powder, pepper and cayenne.
2. Place the steaks on an oiled baking tray. Spread the mayonnaise over the steaks. Sprinkle with half of the rosemary
3. Separate the onion rings and spread over the meat. Sprinkle with the remaining rosemary. Bake for approximately about 40 minutes until the pork is cooked.

Nutritional Value: Calories 418; Fat 24.8g; Carbohydrates 10.2g; Protein 39.8g

Recipe 83: Salmon with Lemon

Serving Size: 6

Cooking Time: 20 minutes

Ingredients:

- 6 salmon fillets - about 1½ pounds.
- 1-oz. parsley, chopped.
- 6 slices lemon
- 3 cloves garlic, finely chopped.
- 6-tablespoon butter, at room temperature.
- Salt and pepper

Directions:

1. Pre heat your oven to the 375 degree °F. Cut 6 pieces of foil large enough to wrap around each piece of fish
2. Mix together the butter, garlic and parsley in a small bowl. Place a salmon fillet in the centre of each piece of foil and season with pepper and salt.
3. Make a few cuts in each salmon fillet with a sharp knife and rub the butter evenly among the pieces
4. Place the lemon slices on top of the fish. Wrap up the 'parcels' and seal the foil at the edges.
5. Place on a baking tray and bake for 12 to 15 minutes in the hot oven. Open the packets to serve piping hot.

Nutritional Value: Calories 258; Fat 18.6g; Carbohydrates 1.5g; Protein 22.4g

Recipe 84: Sausage with Crisp Cabbage

Serving Size: 4

Cooking Time: 10 minutes

Ingredients:

- 4-cups green cabbage, coarsely chopped.
- 12-oz. pure meat pork sausage.
- 4-oz. onion, sliced.
- 2-tablespoon bacon fat.
- 1 large red bell pepper, chopped.
- Salt and pepper

Directions:

1. Skin the sausage and fry in a large skillet, breaking the meat up as it cooks. As the sausage is browning add the onion and allow to cook until soft and translucent
2. Now, add the bacon fat, bell pepper and seasoning. Sauté for a short while longer
3. Add the cabbage and stir fry until it just begins to soften but still retains some crispness. Season to taste and serve.

Nutritional Value: Calories 360; Fat 30.4g; Carbohydrates 9.1g; Protein 10.7g

Recipe 85: Scallops with Moroccan Spices

Serving Size: 4

Cooking Time: 10 minutes

Ingredients:

- ¼-cup chopped fresh cilantro.
- 1-lb. sea scallops.
- 2 cloves garlic, crushed.
- ½ lemon
- 2-tablespoon butter
- 2-tablespoon olive oil.
- 1-teaspoon ground cumin.
- ½-teaspoon ground ginger
- 2-teaspoon paprika.
- ½-teaspoon hot sauce

Directions:

1. In big, skillet, heat the olive oil and butter over medium heat, and swirl them together. Add the garlic, and let it cook for just a minute, then add the cumin, ginger, paprika, and hot sauce
2. Now, add the scallops, and saute, stirring frequently for about 5 to 7 minutes, or until they're opaque
3. Squeeze the lemon over the scallops, and transfer to 4 serving plates. Scatter a-tablespoon of cilantro over each plate, and serve.

Nutritional Value: Calories 220; Fat 14g; Carbohydrates 5g; Protein 19g

Recipe 86: Shrimp Risotto

Serving Size: 4

Cooking Time: 15 minutes

Ingredients:

- 14 oz. shrimps, peeled and deveined
- 12 oz. cauli rice
- 4 button mushrooms
- ½ lemon
- 4 stalks green onion
- 3 tablespoon ghee butter
- 2 tablespoon coconut oil
- Salt and black pepper to taste

Directions:

1. Preheat the oven to 400F
2. Put a layer of cauli rice on a sheet pan, season with salt and spices; sprinkle the coconut oil over it
3. Bake in the oven for 10-12 minutes
4. Cut the green onion, slice up the mushrooms and remove the rind from the lemon
5. Heat the ghee butter in a skillet over medium heat. Add the shrimps; season it and sauté for 5-6 minutes
6. Top the cauli rice with the shrimps, sprinkle the green onion over it.

Nutritional Value: Calories 363; Fat 26.2g; Carbohydrates 9.2g; Protein 25g

Recipe 87: Spiced Lamb Kebabs

Serving Size: 4

Cooking Time: 20 minutes

Ingredients:

- 4 cloves garlic, minced
- 1 small onion, finely chopped.
- 1-lb. lamb, ground.
- 1 fresh egg
- 2-tablespoon coconut flour.
- 6-tablespoon coconut oil
- 1-tablespoon salt
- 1 jalapeño pepper, finely chopped. and seeded.
- ½-teaspoon each of ground cumin, clove, cinnamon, black pepper, chili powder and nutmeg

Directions:

1. In a large-sized bowl mix together all of the ingredients, except the coconut oil. Refrigerate overnight. Form the meat into 8 sausage shapes and press onto 4 metal skewers
2. Melt the coconut oil and brush the meat before placing on a hot grill. Turn often and brush with more oil as needed.
3. 8 to 10 minutes should be sufficient for them to cook and brown. Serve while hot.

Nutritional Value: Calories 430; Fat 30.2g; Carbohydrates 4.9g; Protein 34.1g

Recipe 88: Swordfish and Mango Salsa

Serving Size: 2

Cooking Time: 10 minutes

Ingredients:

- 2 medium swordfish steaks
- Salt and black pepper to the taste
- 2 teaspoons avocado oil
- 1 tablespoon cilantro, chopped
- 1 mango, chopped
- 1 avocado, pitted, peeled and chopped
- A pinch of cumin
- A pinch of onion powder
- A pinch of garlic powder
- 1 orange, peeled and sliced
- ½ balsamic vinegar

Directions:

1. Season fish steaks with salt, pepper, garlic powder, onion powder and cumin.
2. Heat up a large-sized pan with half of the oil over medium high eat, add fish steaks and cook them for 3 minutes on each side.
3. Meanwhile, in a bowl, mix avocado with mango, cilantro, balsamic vinegar, salt, pepper and the rest of the oil and stir well.
4. Divide fish on plates, top with mango salsa and serve with orange slices on the side.
5. Enjoy!

Nutritional Value: Calories 160; Fat 3g; Carbohydrates 4g; Protein 8g

Recipe 89: Turkey and Tomatoes

Serving Size: 4

Cooking Time: 30 minutes

Ingredients:

- 2 shallots, chopped
- 1 tablespoon ghee, melted
- 1 cup chicken stock
- 1 pound turkey breast, cubed
- 1 cup cherry tomatoes, halved
- A pinch of salt and black pepper
- 1 tablespoon rosemary, chopped

Directions:

1. Heat up a large-sized pan with the ghee over medium high heat, add the shallots and the meat and brown for 5 minutes.
2. Add the rest of the prepared ingredients, bring to a simmer and cook over medium heat for 25 minutes, stirring often.
3. Divide into bowls and serve.

Nutritional Value: Calories 150; Fat 4g; Carbohydrates 3g; Protein 10g

Recipe 90: Veal Picatta

Serving Size: 2

Cooking Time: 15 minutes

Ingredients:

- 2 tablespoons ghee
- ¼ cup white wine
- ¼ cup chicken stock
- 1 and ½ tablespoons capers
- 1 garlic clove, minced
- 8 ounces veal scallops
- Salt and black pepper to the taste

Directions:

1. Heat up a large-sized pan with half of the butter over medium high heat, add veal cutlets, season with salt and pepper, cook for 1 minute on each side and transfer to a plate.
2. Heat up the large-sized pan again over medium heat, add garlic, stir and cook for 1 minute.
3. Add wine, stir and simmer for 2 minutes.
4. Add stock, capers, salt, pepper, the rest of the ghee and return veal to pan.
5. Stir everything, cover pan and cook piccata on medium low heat until veal is tender.
6. Enjoy!

Nutritional Value: Calories 204; Fat 12g; Carbohydrates 5g; Protein 10g

Chapter 4:   Dessert Recipes

Recipe 91: Blueberry Tart

Serving Size: 4

Cooking Time: 45 minutes

Ingredients:

- 4 eggs
- 2 teaspoon coconut oil
- 2 cups blueberries
- 1 cup coconut milk
- 1 cup almond flour
- ¼ cup sweetener
- ½ teaspoon vanilla powder
- 1 tablespoon powdered sweetener
- A pinch of salt

Directions:

1. Preheat oven to a heat of 350 F.
2. Place all ingredients except coconut oil, berries, and powdered sweetener in a blender, and blend until smooth.
3. Gently fold in the berries.
4. Pour the mixture into a greased dish and bake for 35 minutes.
5. Sprinkle with powdered sweetener.

Nutritional Value: Calories 355; Fat 14.5g; Carbohydrates 6.9g; Protein 12g

Recipe 92: Butter Delight

Serving Size: 16

Cooking Time: 5 minutes

Ingredients:

- 4 ounces coconut butter
- 4 ounces cocoa butter
- ¼ cup swerve
- ½ cup peanut butter
- 4 ounces dark chocolate, sugar free
- ½ teaspoon vanilla extract
- 1/8 teaspoon xantham gum

Directions:

1. Put all butters and swerve in a pan and heat up over medium heat.
2. Stir until they all combine and then mix with xantham gum and vanilla extract.
3. Stir well again, pour into a lined baking sheet and spread well.
4. Keep this in the fridge for 10 minutes.
5. Heat up a pan with water over medium high heat and bring to a simmer.
6. Add a bowl on top of the pan and add chocolate to the bowl.
7. Stir until it melts and drizzle this over butter mix.
8. Keep in the fridge until everything is firm, cut into 16 pieces and serve.
9. Enjoy!

Nutritional Value: Calories 176; Fat 15g; Carbohydrates 5g; Protein 3g

Recipe 93: Chocolate Almond Squares

Serving Size: 10

Cooking Time: 55 minutes

Ingredients:

- 1/2 cup coconut flour
- 1/2 cup almond meal
- 1 cup almond butter
- 1/4 cup erythritol
- 2 tablespoons coconut oil
- 1/2 cup sugar-free bakers' chocolate, chopped into small chunks

Directions:

1. Mix the coconut flour, almond meal, butter, and erythritol until smooth.
2. Press the mixture into a parchment-lined square pan. Place in your freezer for 30 minutes.
3. Meanwhile, microwave the coconut oil and bakers' chocolate for 40 seconds. Pour the glaze over the cake and transfer to your freezer until the chocolate is set or about 20 minutes.
4. Cut into squares and enjoy!

Nutritional Value: Calories 234; Fat 25.1g; Carbohydrates 2.2g; Protein 1.7g

Recipe 94: Cinnamon Roll Scones

Serving Size: 4

Cooking Time: 40 minutes

Ingredients:

- 2 cups almond flour
- 6 tablespoon swerve sugar, divided
- 2 teaspoon baking powder
- ½ teaspoon salt
- 1 large egg
- ¼ cup unsalted butter, melted
- 2 tablespoon heavy cream
- ½ teaspoon vanilla extract
- 2 teaspoon cinnamon powder

For the glaze:
- 1 tablespoon swerve confectioner's sugar
- 1 oz cream cheese softened
- 1 tablespoon heavy cream
- ¼ teaspoon vanilla extract

Directions:

1. Preheat oven to a heat of 350 F; line a baking sheet with parchment paper.
2. In a bowl, mix almond flour, swerve, baking powder, and salt until well mixed. in another bowl, mix egg, butter, heavy cream, vanilla, and cinnamon powder.
3. Combine both mixtures until smooth. Pour and spread the mixture on the sheet. Cut into 8 wedges and bake for 20 minutes until set and golden.
4. Remove from the oven and let cool. in a bowl, whisk cream cheese, heavy cream, swerve sugar, and vanilla. Swirl the glaze over the scones.

Nutritional Value: Calories 156; Fat 15.4g; Carbohydrates 1.9g; Protein 3g

Recipe 95: Lemon Pudding Cake

Serving Size: 6

Cooking Time: 3 hours

Ingredients:

- 3 eggs, separated.
- 1 ½ cups heavy cream
- ¼-cup almond flour.
- ¼-cup lemon juice.
- 15 packets stevia
- 1-tablespoon butter
- 1-teaspoon grated lemon peel.
- ⅛-teaspoon salt

Directions:

1. Beat egg whites until stiff peaks form. Set aside. Beat egg yolks. Blend in lemon peel, lemon juice, butter and heavy cream
2. In a separate bowl, combine stevia, almond flour and salt. Add to egg-lemon mixture, beating until smooth. Fold into beaten egg whites
3. Spoon into slow cooker. Cover and cook on High 2 to 3 hours.

Nutritional Value: Calories 286; Fat 28g; Carbohydrates 4g; Protein 6g

Recipe 96: Mixed Berry Nuts Mascarpone Bowl

Serving Size: 4

Cooking Time: 10 minutes

Ingredients:

- 4 cups Greek yogurt
- Liquid stevia to taste
- 1 ½ cups mascarpone cheese
- 1 ½ cups blueberries and raspberries
- 1 cup toasted pecans

Directions:

1. Mix the yogurt, stevia, and mascarpone in a bowl until evenly combined.
2. Divide the mixture into 4 bowls, share the berries and pecans on top of the cream.
3. Serve the dessert immediately

Nutritional Value: Calories 480; Fat 40g; Carbohydrates 5g; Protein 20g

Recipe 97: Peanut Butter Bars

Serving Size: 8

Cooking Time: 10 minutes

Ingredients:

For the peanut butter filling:
- ½ cup smooth peanut butter
- 4 tablespoon melted butter
- 4 tablespoon swerve sugar
- 5 tablespoon almond flour
- 1 teaspoon vanilla extract

For the coating:
- 2 ½ oz chopped dark chocolate
- A handful peanuts, chopped

Directions:

1. Line a baking sheet with parchment paper. in a bowl, mix peanut butter, butter, swerve, flour, and vanilla.
2. Spread the mixture onto the sheet and top with chocolate and peanuts.
3. Refrigerate until firm, for 1 hour.
4. Cut into bars and enjoy.

Nutritional Value: Calories 155; Fat 12g; Carbohydrates 5.2g; Protein 4.9g

Recipe 98: Raspberry Custard

Serving Size: 6

Cooking Time: 4 hours

Ingredients:

- 2 cups red raspberries, fresh or frozen, thawed and drained.
- ¾-cup almond flour.
- 12-oz. can evaporated milk
- 5 eggs
- ¼-cup erythritol.
- 2-tablespoon butter
- ½-teaspoon salt
- 1-teaspoon vanilla extract.
- pinch cinnamon

Directions:

1. Beat eggs, erythritol and salt in mixing bowl until eggs no longer cling to whisk. Add flour in three portions, whisking well after each addition until no lumps remain
2. Whisk in evaporated milk, vanilla and cinnamon. Use butter to generously grease slow cooker.
3. Pour egg mixture into cooker. Sprinkle evenly with raspberries. Cover and cook on Low for approximately about 3 to 4 hours, until set
4. Remove lid and allow to cool for 30 to 60 minutes before serving. May chill before serving as well. Variation: Of course, you can use other berries in this custard, whatever you have in the freezer or find to pick.

Nutritional Value: Calories 273; Fat 19g; Carbohydrates 22g; Protein 13g

Recipe 99: Ricotta Mousse

Serving Size: 10

Cooking Time: 0 minutes

Ingredients:

- ½ cup hot coffee
- 2 cups ricotta cheese
- 2 and ½ teaspoons gelatin
- 1 teaspoon vanilla extract
- 1 teaspoon espresso powder
- 1 teaspoon vanilla stevia
- A pinch of salt
- 1 cup whipping cream

Directions:

1. In a bowl, mix coffee with gelatin, stir well and leave aside until coffee is cold.
2. In a bowl, mix espresso, stevia, salt, vanilla extract and ricotta and stir using a mixer.
3. Add coffee mix and stir everything well.
4. Add whipping cream and blend mixture again.
5. Divide into dessert bowls and serve after you've kept it in the fridge for 2 hours.
6. Enjoy!

Nutritional Value: Calories 160; Fat 13g; Carbohydrates 2g; Protein 7g

Recipe 100:   Vanilla Chocolate Mousse

Serving Size: 3

Cooking Time: 30 minutes

Ingredients:

- 3 eggs
- 1 cup dark chocolate chips
- 1 cup heavy cream
- 1 cup fresh strawberries, sliced
- 1 vanilla extract
- 1 tablespoon swerve

Directions:

1. Melt the chocolate in a bowl, in your microwave for a minute on high, and let it cool for 10 minutes.
2. Meanwhile, in a medium-sized mixing bowl, whip the cream until very soft. Add the eggs, vanilla extract, and swerve; whisk to combine. Fold in the cooled chocolate. Divide the mousse between four glasses, top with the strawberry slices and chill in the fridge for at least 30 minutes before serving.

Nutritional Value: Calories 370; Fat 25g; Carbohydrates 3.7g; Protein 7.6g

Chapter 5:   28-Day Meal Plan

Day	Breakfast	Lunch	Dinner
1	Bell Peppers and Avocado Bowls	Coconut Pork and Celery	Lean and Green Broccoli Alfredo
2	Coleslaw with Eggs	Lavender Lamb Chops	Cashew Chicken Curry
3	Egg and Bacon Stuffed Avocados	Seared Scallops and Roasted Grapes	Pork with Mayonnaise
4	Avocado Boats with Tuna Mayo	Bacon Wrapped Chicken	Cheesy Ham with Cauliflower Mash
5	Creamy Eggs	Garlic Pork and Zucchinis	Pork Schnitzel
6	Cauliflower Patties	Spicy Chicken Leg Quarters	Baked Calamari and Shrimp
7	Zucchini and Bacon Hash	Rosemary Pork	Cuba Steak with Onions
8	Breakfast Buttered Eggs	Chicken Wings with Thyme Chutney	Lamb with Fennel and Figs
9	Kale Frittata	Mozzarella Chicken	Salmon with Lemon
10	Cheese and Aioli Eggs	Tangy Chicken Drumsticks	Bacon Wrapped Sausages
11	Sausage Stuffed Bell Peppers	Beef with Kale and Leeks	Scallops with Moroccan Spices
12	Almond Pancakes	Meatballs and Pilaf	Nutmeg Beef Bowls
13	Cheesy Ham and Chive Roll-Ups	Sausage with Tomatoes and Cheese	Oven-Baked Sole Fillets
14	Breakfast Meatloaf	Steak with Blueberry Sauce	Sausage with Crisp Cabbage
15	Feta Omelet	Beef Curry	Chicken and Garlic Green Beans
16	Bacon and Lemon Breakfast Muffins	Oregano Pork Chops	Onions with Spicy Sausage

17	Hot Dog Rolls	Chicken Calzone	Crusted Lamb Chops
18	Cauliflower Omelet	Trout and Endives	Chicken and Mushrooms
19	Spicy Egg Muffins with Bacon and Cheese	Portobello Mushroom with Sausage and Cheese	Shrimp Risotto
20	Basil Mozzarella Eggs	Chicken and Bacon Pie	Baked Sausage and Kale
21	Spicy Scrambled Eggs	Tender Chicken Thighs	Orange Chili Lobster
22	Cheese and Oregano Muffins	Baked Tofu with Roasted Peppers	Spiced Lamb Kebabs
23	Mushroom and Cheese Lettuce Wraps	Parsley Pork and Beef Meatballs	Cod with Bok Choy
24	Shrimp and Olives Pan	Thyme Beef and Leeks	Bell Peppers and Sausage
25	Baked Granola	Sage Beef	Orange Glazed Salmon
26	Ricotta Cloud Pancakes with Whipped Cream	Zucchini Quiche with Pancetta	Turkey and Tomatoes
27	Chili Bacon and Eggs	Beef with Kale and Leeks	Barbecued Pork Chops
28	Brussels Sprouts Delight	Veal Parmesan	Chicken Pasta

8. Conclusion

A Keto diet may be a healthier option for certain people, although the amount of fat, carbohydrates, and protein prescribed varies from person to person. If you have diabetes, talk to the doctor before starting the diet because it would almost certainly need prescription changes and stronger blood sugar regulation. If you're breastfeeding, you shouldn't follow a ketogenic diet. Be mindful that limiting carbs will render you irritable, hungry, and sleepy, among other things. However, this may be a one-time occurrence. Keep in mind that you can eat a balanced diet in order to obtain all of the vitamins and minerals you need. A sufficient amount of fiber is also needed. When the body begins to derive energy from accumulated fat rather than glucose, it is said to be in ketosis. This diet, on the other hand, can be difficult to stick to and can exacerbate health issues in individuals who have certain disorders, such as diabetes type 1. The Keto diet is suitable for the majority of citizens. Nonetheless, all major dietary modifications should be discussed with a dietitian or doctor. This is essentially the case with people who have inherent conditions.

The Keto diet may be an effective therapy for people with drug-resistant epilepsy. Though the diet may be beneficial to people of any age, teenagers, people over 50, and babies can profit the most because they can easily stick to it. Modified Keto diets, such as the revised Atkins diet or the low-glycemic index diet, are safer for adolescents and adults. A doctor and dietitian will maintain track of a person's progress, administer drugs, and test for side effects. The body absorbs fat and protein differently than it does carbohydrates. Carbohydrates have a high insulin reaction. The protein sensitivity to insulin is mild, and the quick insulin response is negligible. If you wish to lose weight, consume as many eggs, chickens, fish, and birds as you want, satiate yourself with the fat, and then eat every vegetable that grows on the ground. Butter and coconut oil can be used instead of processed synthetic seed oils. You may be either a sugar or a fat burner, but not both.

9. Index

Made in the USA
Coppell, TX
01 November 2022

85609646R00063